Formal T̶h̶e̶o̶r̶i̶e̶s̶ ̶o̶f̶ ̶Truth

FORMAL THEORIES OF TRUTH

JC BEALL
MICHAEL GLANZBERG
DAVID RIPLEY

OXFORD
UNIVERSITY PRESS

OXFORD

UNIVERSITY PRESS

Great Clarendon Street, Oxford, OX2 6DP,
United Kingdom

Oxford University Press is a department of the University of Oxford.
It furthers the University's objective of excellence in research, scholarship,
and education by publishing worldwide. Oxford is a registered trade mark of
Oxford University Press in the UK and in certain other countries

Published in the United States of America by Oxford University Press
198 Madison Avenue, New York, NY 10016, United States of America

British Library Cataloguing in Publication Data
Data available

Library of Congress Control Number: 2017959733

ISBN 978-0-19-881567-9 (hbk.)
978-0-19-881568-6 (pbk.)

Printed and bound by
CPI Group (UK) Ltd, Croydon, CR0 4YY

To Chippa, CC, and Harry

CONTENTS

PREFACE

This book was first sketched long ago. The initial idea was to do an exhaustive critical survey of extant formal theories of truth. We now believe that project to be too big to do or too big to be useful to readers. It's a jungle out there—an important and intriguing jungle, but one too vast and thick for this trio to productively map.

An early version of some of this material wound up in the *Stanford Encyclopedia of Philosophy* entry on the liar paradox; and we have maintained some overlap with that entry.

What we hope is that this book serves as a bridge for those philosophers or budding philosophers—or researchers in other disciplines—with a little bit of formal-logic training (even a first course in logic) who wish to take a first step into so-called formal theories of truth. We give enough logical and mathematical tools to wade through simplified pictures of representative formal theories of truth. And that's really our aim: to give a very simple but representative idea of leading formal theories of truth. Mastering this book puts one in position to tackle the details of actual formal theories of truth, in all their richness and complexity.

ACKNOWLEDGMENTS

We are grateful to a great number of amazing people. On the personal side: We keep that personal. On the professional side: some philosophers have been particularly helpful over the years in discussing parts of this book. Among those are Eduardo Barrio, Ross Brady, Mark Colyvan, Roy Cook, Aaron Cotnoir, Elena Ficara, Hartry Field, Chris Gauker, Patrick Greenough, Patrick Grim, Volker Halbach, Richard Heck, Ole Hjortland, Michael Hughes, Dominic Hyde, Carrie Jenkins, Øystein Linnebo, Michael Lynch, Ed Mares, Colin McCullough-Benner, Vann McGee, Chris Mortensen, Julien Murzi, Daniel Nolan, Charles Parsons, Graham Priest, Agustín Rayo, Stephen Read, Greg Restall, Marcus Rossberg, Gill Russell, Josh Schechter, Lionel Shapiro, Stewart Shapiro, Gabriel Uzquiano, Zach Weber, and Crispin Wright.

Colin McCullough-Benner, Matthias Jenny, and Julien Murzi deserve very special thanks for providing substantial feedback on earlier drafts of this book.

Two anonymous OUP reviewers gave very helpful feedback on an early draft of this book. An early version of some of this material wound up in the *Stanford Encyclopedia of Philosophy* entry on the Liar paradox.

Jc is grateful to both the University of Connecticut (Storrs) and the University of Tasmania (Hobart) for research support.

Michael is grateful to Northwestern University and the University of California (Davis) for research support.

Dave is grateful to the University of Connecticut (Storrs) for research support.

Jc & Michael & Dave
Storrs/Hobart & Chicago & Storrs

CHAPTER ONE

Introduction

Truth is one of the oldest and most central topics in philosophy. What it is for something to be true, along with such questions as how we might know what is true, and where fundamentally truth applies, are among the most basic questions that philosophers wrestle with.

Such a broad and fundamental topic as truth may be approached from many different angles. Metaphysics, in more or less traditional forms, has from time to time made the notion of truth itself a central topic. This was evident in the classical period, in the middle ages, and more recently in the early days of the twentieth century, especially in the emergence of "analytic philosophy" in Russell and Moore's response to British idealism, and many subsequent developments.[1]

Developments in logic and thinking about truth have often gone together. They did so in the classical period, where logic as we know it and important ideas about truth emerged; they did so in the medieval period; and in the early days of the twentieth century. They also have done so more recently, starting with work

[1] For an overview of these and many other issues, and many references, see the papers in Glanzberg (2018).

of Tarski (1935). In the years following Tarski, a huge number of developments in formal theories of truth have occurred. That is the topic of this book.

There are a number of reasons the study of logic and truth go together, and have done so for such a long time. One is that some of the basic principles of truth sometimes seem to have the kind of self-evident form, or obviousness, that principles of logic do. If you claim that it is true that Chicago is north of Storrs, then you can claim that Chicago is north of Storrs, and vice versa. What could be more obvious, and what could be more fundamental to the notion of truth? Whether or not this is logic proper, it is certainly the kind of fundamental principle which cries out for formalization using the tools of logic. It thus is, and has been, tempting to think about truth using tools developed for formal logic.

Another reason that the study of truth and the study of formal theories have gone together stems from paradox. The simple principles that seem to govern truth turn out to threaten *inconsistency*. This is a consequence of some well-known *paradoxes*, most importantly the *Liar paradox*.

The Liar paradox, as is very well-known, centers around such sentences as one that says of itself that it is false. Such things might seem to be "mere puzzles," in the sense of games one might play. But they are far more. They show that some very basic principles governing truth, indeed, principles so basic and obvious they might look like logic, might turn out to be *false*. This shows us that formal theories of truth are surprisingly complex, compared to the obvious principles we might first consider.

Because of this situation, formal theories of truth form a rich and complex topic in their own right. That is why the topic of this book requires a book at all. But there is another important reason formal theories of truth have become so important for those interested in logic. Given the seeming obviousness of basic principles of truth, the fact that they lead to inconsistency if we make some background assumptions about logic creates a kind of dilemma. Either some obvious principles about truth, or some equally obvious principles about logic itself, must go. Resolving this dilemma is one of the main jobs of a formal theory of truth. Either way, the consequences are far-reaching. Such a theory might revise what seemed to be clear and obvious principles applying to a fundamental and metaphysically important concept. Or, such a theory might revise what might have seemed to be basic facts about logic. Either choice is quite momentous, of course. This makes formal theories of truth an important test-bed for thinking about the nature of logic, and how it applies to important and basic concepts.

1.1 Our goals in the book

Our goal in this book is to provide a *concise* overview of the main issues, and the main ideas, in formal theories of truth, along with a few key logical techniques such formal theories rely on. We pause to stress that we are not offering a comprehensive survey of work on formal theories of truth. Such a survey would not only be long, complex, and cumbersome; it would involve a huge range of mathematical techniques. Though we believe such a survey would be of great use to specialists, our aim is different. We aim to show enough representatives of the basic ideas and issues—sometimes somewhat simplified representatives—to make clear what the issues are, what is involved in studying them, and why they are significant.

We hope our readers will gain from this book a good understanding of what the field is, and an appreciation of some of the key points in the current and classic literature. This, we hope, will help those whose main interest is not logic to appreciate the place of formal theories in the wider literature on truth. We also hope it will enable those interested in logic and its applications to truth to pursue the rich contemporary literature.

1.2 Basic structure of discussion

In trying to give a useful entry-point into formal theories of truth, we have put clarity and conciseness at the forefront, at the expense of comprehensiveness. We want the book to be a *useful* entry into the field, for both future researchers in the area and for those who simply want a sense of the basic territory, even if the map of terrain is, of necessity, very partial, in perhaps both salient senses of the term.

Each chapter focuses on a *very coarsely individuated* family of approaches to Liar-like paradox. For purposes of clarity, we have tried to structure the main chapters around the following questions:

1. What is the main philosophical motivation or thinking behind the given approach(-es) in the chapter?
2. What does the formal account look like?
3. What are common objections?

Depending on the material at hand, these three themes will appear in various ways. Most of the main chapters have a section, or several sections, on common objections. Most also have sections on formal accounts. They vary on how they separate out philosophical motivations from formal theories, as some theories lend themselves to this more easily than others.

In all cases, readers should be in a position to answer these questions at the end of the given chapters. Indeed, readers can take it as an exercise to answer the questions as explicitly as they can. Sometimes, answers to these exercises will require chasing up some of the cited work; but usually the answers are at hand based on thinking through the chapters.

CHAPTER TWO

Truth-Theoretic Paradoxes
A Select Sampling

Formal theories of truth are interesting and complicated in large part due to the truth-theoretic paradoxes: a subset of the so-called semantic paradoxes. These paradoxes seem to show us that very basic principles governing truth, principles so basic that they might even be principles of logic, are false, or even inconsistent. It is this surprising situation that launches us on our search for ways to make sense of truth formally: a search that leads us to look hard at what kinds of principles govern truth, and at what logic itself really is like.

2.1 Introducing the Liar

Before starting on that search, we should review the problems that get it started: the truth-theoretic paradoxes themselves. These paradoxes have become important guide-posts for formal theories of truth. A good theory must avoid the paradoxes, and how it does so indicates the basic contours of the theory.

We will survey a few of the most important truth-theoretic paradoxes. We will focus especially on those we will refer to as the book proceeds. This is by no means a comprehensive survey.[1]

The truth-theoretic paradoxes emerge easily. We just need a sentence like:

The displayed sentence on page 7 is false.

This sentence is slightly odd. But it is not *that* odd. It could have been written as a note from one author of this book to the others, for instance.

Odd or not, this sort of sentence is remarkable. Some philosophers have thought that *everything*—your worst nightmare, your most precious dreams—follows from the mere existence of sentences like this. This sentence, and its relatives, generate truth-theoretic paradoxes. This one, for instance, is a way of presenting the venerable Liar paradox. Our aim in this chapter is to give a sense of what goes into these paradoxes, and how they work.

To see the basic problem, begin with the displayed sentence on page 7. Observe that the displayed sentence on page 7 is "The displayed sentence on page 7 is false." Observe, too, that the displayed sentence on page 7 says no more nor less than that the displayed sentence on page 7 is false; and so it says of itself that it is false. Something is puzzling here. After all (we might say), every sentence is either true or false, and no sentence is both. Suppose that the displayed sentence on page 7 is true, that is, that "The displayed sentence on page 7 is false" is true. But if "The displayed sentence on page 7 is false" is true, then

---

[1] For more on the range of paradoxes, both truth-theoretic and in related domains, see Cook (2013); Priest (2006b); Sainsbury (2009); Sorensen (2003).

the displayed sentence on page 7 is false; and so if the displayed sentence on page 7 is true, then the displayed sentence on page 7 is false, and so both true and also false. Impossible. On the other option, viz., that the target sentence is false, we get the same problem. If "The displayed sentence on page 7 is false" is false, then the displayed sentence on page 7 is false; and so it is true that the displayed sentence on page 7 is false; and so "The displayed sentence on page 7 is false" is true, and so both false and also true. Impossible.

Now it's clear that the displayed sentence on page 7 engenders a tangled mess of spinning and stretching and looping and more. But why might one think it a *powerful* sentence—one whose mere existence implies everything? The reason invokes logic: in many logical systems, a contradiction (e.g. the claim that the sentence is both true and false) implies everything. If we have to say (on the authority of logic?) that every sentence is either true or false, then we have to say as much about the displayed sentence on page 7. But given the tangled-thicket nature of the displayed sentence on page 7, we wind up saying as a result that it's also both true and false—and hence, our best dreams (and worst nightmares) are true. Something has got to be wrong. We don't know about you, but at least our best dreams (and, fortunately, worst nightmares) aren't true. The question is: what is going wrong in our reasoning about the displayed sentence on page 7? What does it tell us about truth? What of logic? What else?

Such questions are at the heart of this book. But before we get to those questions, we need to understand better what creates the kind of tangled mess we have just seen, in a way we can work with formally. We also need to see a few more instances of the kind of problem we just saw. That will be our focus for the remainder of this chapter.

Historical note. The puzzle we have just reviewed, and will explore more in the following, is usually known as the *Liar paradox*. It is a paradox, as we have observed, as it seems to lead us to contradictions, and all the problems they bring with them. It is the Liar paradox, as the displayed sentence on page 7 in effect says of itself that it is not true, i.e., that it is a lie.

That there is some sort of puzzle to be found with sentences like that one has been noted frequently throughout the history of philosophy. It was discussed in classical times, notably by the Megarians, but it was also mentioned by Aristotle and by Cicero. As one of the insolubilia, it was the subject of extensive investigation by medieval logicians such as Bradwardine and Buridan. More recently, work on this problem has been an integral part of the development of modern mathematical logic, and it has become a subject of extensive research in its own right. The paradox is sometimes called the "Epimenides paradox" as the tradition attributes a sentence like the first one in this essay to Epimenides of Crete, who is reputed to have said that all Cretans are always liars. That some Cretan has said so winds up in no less a source than the New Testament (Titus 1:12)![2]   *End historical note*

2.2 Simple-falsity Liar

The way we introduced the Liar paradox, with a displayed sentence, is not the most convenient way to work with it formally. We can simplify it somewhat by using a sentence that talks about itself more

---

[2] Thus, a paradox nearly occurs in the New Testament. For a delightful discussion, see Anderson (1970). For a more thorough discussion of the history of the Liar, see Sorensen (2003). There has been some important recent work on medieval theories of the Liar, and their relevance to current approaches. For instance, see Read (2002, 2006); Restall (2008); Simmons (1993), and the papers in Rahman *et al.* (2008).

directly. Consider a sentence named "FLiar," which says of itself (i.e., says of FLiar) that it is false.

(FLiar)   FLiar is false.

This is the same sort of sentence as the displayed sentence on page 7. FLiar, like the displayed sentence on page 7, seems to lead to contradiction as follows. If the sentence "FLiar is false" is true, then FLiar is false. But if FLiar is false, then the sentence "FLiar is false" is true. Since FLiar just is the sentence "FLiar is false," we have it that FLiar is false if and only if FLiar is true. But, now, if every sentence is true or false, FLiar itself is either true or false, in which case—given our reasoning previous—it is both true and false. This is a contradiction. Contradictions, according to many logical theories (e.g., classical logic, intuitionistic logic, and plenty of others), imply absurdity—triviality, that is, that every sentence is true.

2.3   Simple-untruth Liar

We can simplify FLiar in another way. We do not really need to work with falsehood. Instead, we can construct a Liar sentence with the complex predicate "not true."[3] Consider a sentence named "ULiar" (for "un-true"), which says of itself that it is not true.

(ULiar)   ULiar is not true.

The argument towards contradiction is similar to the FLiar case. In short: if ULiar is true, then it is not true; and if not true, then true. But, now, if every sentence is either true or not true, ULiar itself is

[3] Terminology here is not uniform. In van Fraassen (1968) the term "strengthened Liar" is introduced to name what we are calling the simple-untruth Liar. Van Fraassen's term, however, has been more often used for a "revenge-like" paradox in the manner of Parsons (1974), as we discuss in Chapter 6.

either true or not true, in which case it is both true and not true. This is a contradiction.

As we will see in what follows, there is a sense in which ULiar is more powerful than FLiar. To anticipate, if you thought that the way to respond to the Liar is to simply declare it to be neither true nor false, you will have to work much harder to explain what is happening with ULiar than with FLiar.

2.4 Liar cycles

One might think that explicit self-reference is required for any version of the Liar paradox. Not so.

Consider a very concise (viz., one-sentence-each) dialog between siblings Max and Agnes.

> Max: Agnes's claim is true.
> Agnes: Max's claim is not true.

What Max said is true if and only if what Agnes said is true. But what Agnes said (viz., "Max's claim is not true") is true if and only if what Max said is not true. Hence, what Max said is true if and only if what Max said is not true. But, now, if what Max said is true or not true, then it is both true and not true. And this, as in the FLiar and ULiar cases, is a contradiction, implying, according to many logical theories, absurdity.

2.5 Boolean compounds

Liar paradoxes can also be formed using more complex sentence structure, rather than complex modes of reference. One that has been important involves so-called Boolean compounds. These can enter into Liar-like sentences in many ways. One particularly sticky one is as follows. Consider the following sentence named "DLiar" (for "Disjunctive"):

(DLiar) Either DLiar is not true or a wombat once ran at 45km/h.

Now, we have no idea whether a wombat ever ran at 45km/h. Nor, we think, does anyone else. Wombats have been recorded up around 40km/h, so it's not impossible that one once ran at 45km/h. But probably nobody was around to clock it if it did. Nonetheless, using DLiar, we can "prove" that a wombat once ran at 45km/h.

Suppose DLiar isn't true. Then "DLiar is not true" is true, and since DLiar is a disjunction with a true disjunct, it's true. But this is a contradiction, since we're supposing it's not true. By so-called reductio, we can conclude that DLiar is true. So either DLiar is not true or a wombat once ran at 45km/h. But it can't be that DLiar is not true, since we've concluded that it's true. So a wombat once ran at 45km/h.

Maybe that's a perfectly true conclusion, and maybe it's not. (Again, we don't know, and we don't think anyone does.) Clearly, though, nobody should believe it on the basis of this reasoning. The mere existence of DLiar is enough to run that argument. Even if there were no wombats, or they all moved very slowly, we could give just the same argument. Moreover, you can replace "a wombat once ran at 45km/h" with any declarative sentence you want in this reasoning, and you'll have a "proof" of that sentence, no matter how obviously or necessarily false it is.

We mention DLiar because it's connected with another important paradox: Curry's paradox. This involves conditionals that say of themselves only that if they (the conditionals themselves) are true, then so too is some other sentence (as in this case, the other sentence can be anything you like). At least in languages where the conditional is the material conditional, and so $A \supset B$ is equivalent to $\neg A \vee B$, DLiar is equivalent to the Curry sentence "DLiar is true $\supset$ a wombat once ran at 45km/h."

This gives a peek at Curry's paradox, but you should note that Curry's paradox is most important where the conditional is different from the material conditional (or some modalized variant of it). In such settings, the Curry paradox does not depend on negation, as DLiar does.[4]

2.6 Infinite sequences

The question of whether the Liar paradox really requires some sort of circularity has been the subject of extensive debate. Liar cycles (e.g., the Max–Agnes dialog) show that explicit self-reference is not necessary, but it is clear that such cycles involve circular reference. Yablo (1993b) has argued that a more complicated kind of multi-sentence paradox produces a Liar without circularity.

Yablo's paradox relies on an infinite sequence of claims $A_0, A_1, A_2, \ldots$, where each A_i says that all of the "greater" A_k (i.e., the A_k such that $k > i$) are untrue. In other words, each claim says of the later claims that they're all untrue. Since we have an infinite sequence, this version of the Liar paradox appears to avoid the sort of circularity apparent in the previous examples; it's a line not a circle. However, contradiction still seems to emerge. If A_0 is true, then all of the "greater" A_k are untrue, and a fortiori A_1 is untrue. But, then, there is at least one true A_k greater than A_1 (i.e., some A_k such that $k > 1$), which contradicts A_0. Conversely, if A_0 is untrue, then there's at least one true A_k greater than A_0. Letting A_m be such a one (i.e., a truth greater than A_0), we have it that A_{m+1} is

---

[4] For more on the Curry paradox, see Beall (2008a).

untrue, in which case there's some truth greater than A_{m+1}. But this contradicts A_m. What we have, then, is that if A_0 (the first claim in the infinite sequence) is true or untrue, then it is both. And this, as in the other cases, is a contradiction.

Whether Yablo's paradox really avoids self-reference has been much debated. See, for instance, Barrio (2012); Beall (2001); Cook (2006, 2014); Priest (1997); Sorensen (1998) and references therein. It also raises the question of which patterns of reference among sentences can give rise to paradox; for exploration of this issue, see Cook (2014); Rabern *et al.* (2013).

2.7 On paradoxes beyond the Liar

Logic, and philosophy more generally, from time to time focuses on paradoxes of many different sorts. For instance, Zeno's famous paradox seems, absurdly, to threaten the idea that there can be motion. Closer to our subject-matter, the Sorites paradox seems to threaten the coherence of vague predicates, while Russell's (and Zermelo's) paradoxes seem to threaten the coherence of the (naïve) notion of set. Closer still to our main topic, a relative of Russell's paradox applies to notions like property and exemplification. (Example: every predicate is *true of* all and only the objects that *exemplify* the property expressed by the predicate. Now consider the predicate "does not exemplify itself." Does the property expressed by this predicate exemplify itself? It does if and only if it doesn't. Contradiction!) And there are other paradoxes in the vicinity, ones involving notions of reference and definability.

We focus on variants of the Liar paradox because, as we discuss in future chapters, they guide theorizing about truth in substantial ways. Other paradoxes in the vicinity of the Liar also can constrain theories of truth in substantial ways, but perhaps haven't explicitly guided such theories in quite the same way that the Liar paradox has done. What kind of formal theory of truth one may have depends in large measure on how one avoids the Liar paradox.[5]

[5] See the references in footnote 1.

CHAPTER THREE

Ingredients of a Liar

In Chapter 2 we saw some examples of truth-theoretic paradoxes, which were all variants of the Liar paradox. One of the main constraints on formal theories of truth, we saw, was that they must avoid the Liar paradox. To see how that might be done, we need a more formal presentation of the paradox. We will provide one in this chapter.

3.1 Basic ingredients

Our guiding samples of Liar-like paradox, from Chapter 2, share some common ingredients. Our aim in this chapter is to illuminate the common ingredients and common patterns in such samples.

We highlight three aspects of the Liar paradox: the role of truth predicates, the kinds of truth-theoretic principles governing truth predicates, and the way that a paradox can be derived given these resources.

3.1.1 The truth predicate

The first ingredient in building a Liar is a truth predicate, which we write here as T. We follow the usual custom in logic of treating this as a predicate of sentences.[1]

We assume that, along with the truth predicate, we have appropriate names of sentences. For a given sentence A, suppose that $\langle A \rangle$ is a name for it. (This is not automatic, and we need some way of achieving it. For a quick and shallow discussion of some options, see Chapter 4.) $T\langle A \rangle$ is then a predication of truth to A.

We shall say that a predicate T is a *truth predicate for language* $\mathcal{L}$ only if $T\langle A \rangle$ is well-formed for every sentence A of $\mathcal{L}$. But to be a truth predicate for $\mathcal{L}$, the predicate T also needs to obey various principles governing its behavior on sentences of $\mathcal{L}$. It is to such principles that we now turn.

3.1.2 Principles of truth

The tradition, going back to Tarski (1935), has it that the behavior of the truth predicate T is described by the following "schema", which implies the given biconditionals for each sentence A in the language.

$$T\langle A \rangle \leftrightarrow A.$$

This is usually called the *T-schema*, or a T-schema tied to the conditional (the arrow) in question. Tarski himself took the biconditional in question to be the material biconditional $\equiv$ of classical logic, defined via the conjunction of $A \supset B$ and its

---

[1] One could, as some approaches to resolving the paradoxes do, take the primary bearers of truth to be propositions, in which case one would read our notation slightly differently (basically, as a predicate applying to propositions, rather than sentences); but, unless otherwise noted, we follow the standard and convenient route of taking the truth predicate to apply to sentences.

converse $B \supset A$, where these are defined as $\neg A \lor B$ and $\neg B \lor A$, respectively, and all of this is understood via classical logic.

But the Liar paradox has driven much thinking about non-classical logics. The question arises: What principles govern the truth predicate T if—as subsequent chapters discuss—classical logic is rejected, and if, in particular, certain behavior on the part of $\leftrightarrow$ is not guaranteed?

The leading idea for what governs the truth predicate invokes two sorts of principles or "rules" (e.g., two sorts of "inference rules" in some sense). From a sentence A, you can infer $T\langle A \rangle$, that is, you can "capture" A with the truth predicate. Conversely, from $T\langle A \rangle$, you can infer A, that is, you can "release" A from the truth predicate. In some logics, capture and release wind up being equivalent to the T-schema, but it is often helpful to break these up as explicit rules on their own:

- *Capture. A* entails $T\langle A \rangle$. (We also write this as $A \vdash T\langle A \rangle$.)
- *Release.* $T\langle A \rangle$ entails *A*. (We also write this as $T\langle A \rangle \vdash A$.)

Entailment is the relation that holds between the premise(s) and conclusion(s) of a valid argument. There are lots of theories about both the nature and the extension of this relation; for now, we will sidestep these, and just work with entailment in the abstract, using the symbol $\vdash$ to record entailment claims. Capture and release together tell us that every sentence entails, and is entailed by, the claim that it is true.

Capture and release seem, as basic principles should, quite obvious. They might even seem like logical principles in their own right, or something near enough to it. There are other reasons that could be given for them, too. One based on a more substantial claim is that the interderivability of A and $T\langle A\rangle$, i.e., the equivalence of the two, is a *defining characteristic* of truth. We might also note that the T-schema, in a classical interpreted language, suffices to fix the correct extension of T—at least, if the paradoxes can be kept at bay!

3.1.3 *The Liar in short*

The Liar paradox begins with a language $\mathcal{L}$ containing a truth predicate T for $\mathcal{L}$, where T obeys some form of capture and release. We now explore more carefully how a paradox results from these assumptions.

3.1.3.1 EXISTENCE OF LIAR-LIKE SENTENCES

The Liar relies on some form of self-reference: the Liar sentence talks about itself. (More complicated paradoxes, like Liar cycles and Yablo paradoxes, still need some way for sentences to talk about other sentences, and you can read what follows here as covering that as well.)

Natural languages have no trouble generating self-reference. The displayed sentence on page 7 is one example. Self-reference can also be accidental, as in the case where someone writes "The only sentence on the blackboard in room 101 is not true", by chance writing this on the otherwise-blank blackboard in room 101 itself (e.g., Parsons, 1974).

In formal languages, self-reference is also easy to come by. Any language capable of expressing some basic syntax (i.e., talking about the structure of the language in an accurate and sufficiently complete way) can generate self-referential sentences via so-called diagonalization.[2] A language containing a truth predicate and the ability to discuss its own (sufficiently rich) syntax will have a sentence λ such that λ implies $\neg T\langle\lambda\rangle$ and vice versa:

$$\lambda \dashv\vdash \neg T\langle\lambda\rangle.$$

This, in mathematical lingo, is a "fixed point" of (the compound predicate) $\neg T$, and is, in effect, our simple-untruth Liar. λ "says of itself" that it is not true, in that it is equivalent to the statement that it is not true.

Parenthetical remark. It may help some readers (here and throughout) to think of such a Liar sentence λ arising from a *name* c that denotes the sentence $\neg Tc$. In this way, we can think of the existence of the Liar as being reflected in the identity $c = \langle \neg Tc \rangle$. This sometimes takes a bit more to come by in formal languages, but it can still be done in the right kind of setting.

Moreover, it seems to approximate the situation in natural languages: Most natural-language Liar sentences are not just *equivalent* to the claims that they are not true; they *are* the claims that they are not true. For useful discussion, see Heck (2007). *End parenthetical remark.*

3.1.3.2 OTHER LOGICAL "LAWS"

We saw in Chapter 2 that the disastrous conclusions of the Liar paradox follow from arguments, even if those arguments are seemingly tangled and tortuous (if not torturous!). To explore these arguments formally, we will need some logical principles.

---

[2] For some further discussion, see Chapter 4. For more details, see e.g., Boolos (1995) or Smith (2007).

Some of the important principles concern the logical behavior of basic connectives. As before, we read "$A \vdash B$" as that A *entails* B, that the argument from A to B is valid. Important principles for the Liar then include:

- Excluded middle (LEM): $\vdash A \vee \neg A$.
- Explosion (ECQ):[3] $A \wedge \neg A \vdash B$.
- Disjunction principle (DP):[4] If $A \vdash C$ and $B \vdash C$, then $A \vee B \vdash C$.
- Conjunction principle (CP): If $A \vdash B$ and $A \vdash C$, then $A \vdash B \wedge C$.

We will also need some principles governing the behavior of the turnstile $\vdash$ itself, which show us how implication works. For the moment, we will suppose:

- Closure: If A and $A \vdash B$, then B.

We are not suggesting that these are the *only* logical features involved in common Liar paradoxes; but they're arguably the most important of the salient ones.

3.1.3.3 THE LIAR IN ABSTRACT

We now use the foregoing ingredients to provide an abstract form of the paradox, which in turn we use, in subsequent chapters, to locate different responses to the paradox.

We suppose that we have a language $\mathcal{L}$ which contains a truth predicate T for itself, and that $\mathcal{L}$ enjoys enough syntax to have a

---

[3] It is this principle or rule that we repeated by saying that by the lights of many logical theories an arbitrary contradiction implies absurdity or triviality, in the sense of implying all sentences. The principle is sometimes labeled by the classical titles "ex contradictione quodlibet" or "ex falso quodlibet", and hence is often abbreviated "ECQ" or "EFQ" in spite of the name "explosion".

[4] Principles like this are sometimes called "$\vee$-Left", "$\vee$-Out", "$\vee$-Elim", or, more suggestively, "reasoning by cases". It is also the sort of principle or "law" that is sometimes called a "meta-rule" or "meta-law", since it talks about *connections between* claims of entailment, rather than simply providing such a claim.

sentence λ such that $\lambda \dashv\vdash \neg T\langle\lambda\rangle$. We also suppose that the logic of $\mathcal{L}$ obeys LEM, ECQ, DP, CP, and Closure.

The argument that our Liar sentence λ implies a contradiction runs as follows.

1. Showing that $T\langle\lambda\rangle \vdash T\langle\lambda\rangle \wedge \neg T\langle\lambda\rangle$:
   - (a) $T\langle\lambda\rangle$ [premise]
   - (b) λ [1a: release]
   - (c) $\neg T\langle\lambda\rangle$ [1b: definition of λ]
   - (d) $T\langle\lambda\rangle \wedge \neg T\langle\lambda\rangle$ [1a, 1c: CP]
2. Showing that $\neg T\langle\lambda\rangle \vdash T\langle\lambda\rangle \wedge \neg T\langle\lambda\rangle$:
   - (a) $\neg T\langle\lambda\rangle$ [premise]
   - (b) λ [2a: definition of λ]
   - (c) $T\langle\lambda\rangle$ [2b: capture]
   - (d) $T\langle\lambda\rangle \wedge \neg T\langle\lambda\rangle$ [2a, 2c: CP]
3. $T\langle\lambda\rangle \vee \neg T\langle\lambda\rangle \vdash T\langle\lambda\rangle \wedge \neg T\langle\lambda\rangle$ [1, 2: DP]
4. $T\langle\lambda\rangle \wedge \neg T\langle\lambda\rangle$ [3: LEM, Closure]
5. B [4: ECQ, Closure]

Following the above reasoning, B itself turns out to be derivable. But B, here, was totally arbitrary—it could be absolutely anything! In the face of such absurdity, we conclude that something must be wrong in the foregoing Liar reasoning. The question is: what is it? This is the main question that the Liar paradox raises, and it has been given a wide range of answers.

This version of the Liar is one of many.[5] Like any version, it highlights some aspects of the paradox and obscures others.

---

[5] With a little more complexity, for instance, either capture or release can be avoided in favor of some other background assumptions. So-called intuitionistic (i.e., intuitionistic-logic) variants of the Liar are also available, though we shall not explore intuitionistic logic here. For the classical case, Friedman and Sheard (1987) provide a helpful list of inconsistent theories relative to a fairly weak base theory. They show that either of the classical conditional forms of capture or release are inconsistent

We'll use it as our primary derivation going forwards, but we will sometimes have cause to look at other derivations as well.

3.2 Guiding questions

We close this chapter with some questions that guide subsequent chapters.

- Does the Liar tell us something about *logical connectives*—for example, negation or the like? Yes, according to non-classical theories, a sampling of which is given in Chapter 5.
- Does the Liar tell us something about *principles of truth*—and, in particular, restrictions on capture and/or release? Yes, according to classical theories, a sampling of which is given in Chapter 6.
- Does the Liar tell us something else—perhaps about the *deep nature* of logical consequence? Yes, according to substructural theories, a sampling of which is given in Chapter 7.

But before we turn to such approaches we turn to a brief interlude on some of the tools we'll later use.

by themselves, over the base theory supplemented by the right choice of principles providing for completeness or consistency of truth. For an overview of some desiderata often applied to theories of truth, and how the Liar can show them to fail, see Leitgeb (2007).

CHAPTER FOUR

Preliminaries and Technicalities

Subsequently, in this book, we'll begin to look at a variety of formal theories of truth that have been explored by various authors. Before we dive into that, though, we first want to pause to give a bit of background that we will presuppose as we go on. This chapter is that pause.

Here, we explore how names of sentences work in formal languages, and a little of how we can achieve or simulate self-reference for sentences like the Liar sentences. We also talk a bit about how to think about formal languages. We review a number of other things as well: differences between languages and theories, how composition principles can be stated, and how we can define consequence relations for formal languages. If you are not yet familiar with the materials in this chapter, our hope is not to make you an expert (sorry!). We just want to give you enough familiarity to follow the discussions in the rest of the book.

4.1 Truth and satisfaction

When people talk about truth, they do not only concern themselves with which complete sentences are true. Another concern is with which *predicates* are true of which *things*; in other words, which things *satisfy* which predicates. Importantly, sometimes this concern involves complex predicates: open sentences. That is, instead of saying that "Snow is white and cold" is true, we might want to say that "x is white and cold" is *true of* snow, that snow *satisfies* "x is white and cold". This is of both intuitive and formal import.

Satisfaction seems to obey analogues of capture and release. Capture for satisfaction: $A(a)$ entails that a satisfies the open sentence $A(x)$. "Snow is white and cold" entails that snow satisfies "x is white and cold". Release: that a satisfies an open sentence $A(x)$, entails $A(a)$. That snow satisfies "x is white and cold" entails that snow is white and cold. The notion of satisfaction, if subject to these constraints, is just as paradox-prone as the notion of truth. (Ask yourself whether the open sentence "x does not satisfy itself" satisfies itself or not.)

We want not just this one-place notion of satisfaction, but the more general notion of a *sequence* of things satisfying an open sentence. This allows us to consider whether the pair ⟨Sam, Alex⟩ satisfies the open sentence "x_1 loves x_2", whether the triple ⟨Jc, Michael, Dave⟩ satisfies the open sentence "x_1 lives closer to x_2 than x_3 does", etc. (We can then see truth of (closed) sentences as the zero-place version of this.)

Under certain conditions, though, the one-place notion is enough. Sometimes, we can treat these pairs, triples, etc, as things themselves, and ask about closely related open sentences like "x is such that its first member loves its second" and "x is such that its first member lives closer to its second than its third does".

We can't go farther, however: while we can *define* a truth predicate from a satisfaction predicate à la Tarski (1944), taking a sentence to be true iff it is satisfied by every sequence, we cannot go in the other direction. Satisfaction gives us expressive resources we simply don't have if we stick to just truth (unless we assume that everything has a name). Similarly, sometimes theories based on satisfaction are stronger in measurable respects than those based on truth only.

Here, we record our preference for accounts of truth that can extend easily to accounts for satisfaction as well. Since truth and satisfaction seem so closely related, it would be a shame if we had to deal with the paradoxes they engender in radically different ways. But for the next sections, we stick to concerning ourselves with truth alone, and do not comment further on satisfaction. (All of the theories of truth we will consider meet this challenge.)

4.2 Talking about the language

So far, we've written things like $T\langle A\rangle$ for the claim that A is true, without much attention as to how things like that get into the language in the first place. T is easy: it's our distinguished truth predicate. But $\langle A\rangle$ can take a bit of work. It's a term, but where does it come from?

There are a few options available for this sort of thing. In this section, we'll look at three strategies for providing terms for the formulas of our language, and discuss some of the ups and downs of these strategies. Each is in common use, so if you're going to engage the literature on formal theories of truth, it would be good for you to have at least some familiarity with each of these three strategies.

4.2.1 Terms from formulas

The first strategy, which we will call the *terms from formulas* strategy, is probably the simplest.[1] The idea is this: just as connectives, for

---

[1] This strategy is used, for instance, in Kremer (1988).

example ¬, allow us to produce new formulas from old (for each A there is a $\neg A$), and just as function symbols, for example f, allow us to produce new terms from old (for each t there is an $f(t)$), we introduce $\langle\ \rangle$ as a device that allows us to produce new *terms* from old *formulas*.

Just as with connectives and function symbols, $\langle\ \rangle$ on this approach is an ingredient of the language itself. (This is the only one of the three approaches we consider that works this way.) As such, we include a clause to handle $\langle\ \rangle$ in the recursive specification of the language, something like: if A is a formula, then $\langle A \rangle$ is a term, together with the usual (and usually implicit, but no less important for that) requirements of unique readability: if $\langle A \rangle$ is the same term as $\langle B \rangle$, then A is the same formula as B. Constraining our models to deal appropriately with these terms is quite direct: we can simply require each model to include all formulas of the language in its domain,[2] and insist that each $\langle A \rangle$ is interpreted so as to pick out A itself.

One thing to note: this approach does *not*, at least not directly, result in any self-referential sentences. In particular, no formula A can contain $\langle A \rangle$ on this approach. This is for the same reason that no sentence can contain its own negation, in usual propositional languages.[3] Think of the recursive specification of the language as telling us how to build up the language from some starting pieces. Engaging in this metaphor, $\langle A \rangle$ doesn't get constructed until A already exists, so there is no way to get $\langle A \rangle$ into A. More generally, loops are blocked: if, for $0 \leq i < n$, each A_i contains $\langle A_{i+1} \rangle$, then A_n cannot contain $\langle A_0 \rangle$.

---

[2] Thus restricting ourselves to models with infinite domains.

[3] Note that if a sentence *could* contain its own negation, we wouldn't need a truth predicate at all to get paradoxes.

But while no sentence is inherently self-referential on this approach, we can still capture self-reference (and loops and such) by using an equality predicate =. For example, if $l = \langle \neg Tl \rangle$, then $\neg Tl$ is a Liar sentence. It does not contain the term $\langle \neg Tl \rangle$, but it does contain the term l; if = receives its usual interpretation, then for $l = \langle \neg Tl \rangle$ to be true on a model, then l must pick out the same thing as $\langle \neg Tl \rangle$, namely, the formula $\neg Tl$.

Thus, the terms from the formulas approach do not on their own generate self-referential sentences, but they give us enough of a grip on the language to allow certain identity claims to entail self-reference.

4.2.2 Auxiliary function

Another option is what we will call the *auxiliary function* approach.[4] On this approach, we can simply specify the language as usual, with no additional provision for $\langle \rangle$ or anything like it. Then we operate entirely at the level of interpretation. As with the terms from formulas approach, we require that every model includes all formulas of the language in its domain.

Assume (as is usual) that our language has denumerably many primitive terms and denumerably many formulas.[5] Divide the primitive terms into two denumerable stocks. The first stock

[4] This strategy is used, for instance, in Barwise and Etchemendy (1987); Maudlin (2004); Ripley (2012).

[5] Here, we see infinity poke its head in. A collection is *denumerable* iff it has as many members as there are natural numbers. This is the smallest infinity, and it is a usual size for a formal language. Larger infinites, however, can also work here. We need an infinite collection of terms because we need to divide the terms into two disjoint collections with the following properties: the first collection has as many members as both collections combined, and the second collection has as many members as there are formulas in the language. Infinity is what allows us to pull this trick.

we treat as usual; each term simply gets assigned to some member of the domain by each model. The second stock is where the action is. For some bijection τ (the auxiliary function) between the second stock and the formulas of the language, we require each term t from the second stock to refer to the formula $\tau(t)$. Since τ is a bijection, it has an inverse, which we write $\langle\ \rangle$.

Thus, for any formula A, $\langle A \rangle$ is a particular term from the second stock: the term t such that $\tau(t) = A$. "t" and "$\langle A \rangle$" are different terms in *our* language—mathematical English—but they pick out *the very same* object-language term: t and $\langle A \rangle$ are identical (not just required to corefer!). As such, Tt and $T\langle A \rangle$ are also *the very same* object-language sentence. From the point of view of the language itself, $\langle A \rangle$ is just another term: t. But because t is a term from the second stock, its interpretation is constrained by τ: we consider only models that interpret it as referring to A.

By filling in different bijections for τ, we can achieve any pattern of self-reference or looping that we like on this approach; it is more general than the terms from formulas approach. For example, if $\tau(t)$ is $\neg Tt$, then $\neg Tt$ is the very sentence $\neg T\langle\neg Tt\rangle$; it is thus a sentence A that actually contains $\langle A \rangle$, which was impossible on the terms-from-formulas approach. Loops, too, can be generated by appropriate choice of τ.

Because of this, the auxiliary function approach allows us to construct paradoxical sentences *directly*, without needing to depend on the truth of any object-language identity claims. If $\tau(t)$ is $\neg Tt$, then $\neg Tt$ is a Liar sentence. We can even consider self-reference in languages that lack $=$ using this strategy; this is not possible on the terms-from-formulas approach. Of course, if $=$ is present, we can still use it to make claims that force self-reference indirectly as well.

4.2.3 *Arithmetic*

The previous two approaches achieve reference to the language by fiat: we simply require that the formula's language appear in the domain, and insist that certain terms refer to these formulas. They differ only in how they manage the insistence. But there is a subtler way to achieve reference to the language: via arithmetic. Usual developments of this approach work within classical logic, and here we will do the same. (It is not always straightforward to see how to adapt this approach to nonclassical settings, but see Halbach and Horsten (2006); Priest (2003); Restall (1994) for some examples.) We will not present this in any real detail here; we'll just sketch the broad idea. For more in-depth presentations, see e.g., Boolos (1995); Boolos *et al.* (2007); Smith (2007).

Start from a language with a special term $\underline{o}$ for zero, and functions $S, +,$ and $\times$ for successor, addition, and multiplication respectively. We will use this language to talk about natural numbers. Just as $\underline{o}$ is a term for zero, $S\underline{o}$ is a term for one, $SS\underline{o}$ is a term for two, etc; rather than write out long strings of Ss, we will write $\underline{n}$ for the term that precedes $\underline{o}$ with n many Ss. So, $\underline{n}$ is a term for n, for any natural number n; we call these terms *numerals*.

Now, we want to use this language to talk about its own formulas. To do this, we define a function # that takes each formula of the language to a particular natural number. Not just any # will do, but there are many choices that will work. (One vital requirement is that # be one-one, so that it never takes two formulas to the same number—but there are others, as we will soon see.)

Given such an assignment of numbers to formulas, we can now "translate" any relation on formulas into a relation on numbers: the relation that holds between two numbers precisely when those numbers are associated (by #) with formulas connected by the original relation. For example, consider the relation "being the negation of". This holds between formulas A and B exactly when A is $\neg B$. This is translated by the relation on natural numbers that holds between numbers m and n just when there is some formula B such that $m = \#\neg B$ and $n = \#B$, just when the numbers code formulas that stand in the original relation.

This works for any relation at all on formulas. But there are some relations that are important for our purposes here. The simplest examples are the properties (one-place relations) of being a formula, and of being a (closed) sentence. We did not require that every number be $\#A$ for some formula A, and indeed this is not usually done. But we still want to keep track of which numbers *are* the codes of formulas; among these, we want to keep track of which are codes for formulas that are, in addition, sentences. Here we use form and sent as our predicates, with the intention that $\text{form}(\underline{n})$ be true exactly when n is $\#A$ for some formula A, and that $\text{sent}(\underline{n})$ be true when n is $\#A$ for some sentence A.

It turns out that, if we construct $\#$ with enough care, and if we can prove some very simple things about numbers, then we can *define* the predicates form and sent just from the arithmetic materials we already have to hand. Moreover, we can prove $\text{form}(\underline{n})$ iff n is $\#A$ for some formula A, and prove $\neg\text{form}(\underline{n})$ otherwise; and similarly for sent.[6]

But there is much more than just this that we can define, and that we'll have use for. We'll use a unary function $\dot{\neg}$ on natural numbers such that whenever $n = \#A$, then $\dot{\neg}n = \#\neg A$, and similarly a binary function $\dot{\wedge}$ such that whenever $m = \#A$ and

---

[6] This is where much of the detail we're not going into arises. Note that, although there always *is* some relation on numbers answering to any relation on formulas, they are not all definable in this way.

$n = \#B$, then $m \wedge n = \#A \wedge B$, and so for $\vee$, $\supset$. All these are also definable in our arithmetic language, given a suitable choice of # and suitable arithmetic axioms. Again, we can prove the true claims about syntax that are formulable with these tools.

We can likewise deal with quantification, first by extending # to assign numbers to variables as well, and then defining a binary function $\forall$ on natural numbers such that whenever $m = \#v$ for some variable v and $n = \#A$ for a formula A, then $\forall(m, n) = \#\forall vA$, and similarly for $\exists$. These functions, too, are definable, and we can prove the appropriate claims. We also can define a substitution function, so that if $n = \#A$ and $m = \#x$ and $o = \#t$ for a closed term t, then $n(o/m)$ is the code of the result of substituting t for x in A.

So far, we defined all these operations in terms of numbers that code formulas and terms. But we can put this all inside our formal theory of arithmetic, by using the corresponding numerals. Now, we can define $\langle A \rangle$ to be $\underline{\#A}$, i.e., the formal numeral for the code number for A. This is a complex term of the language of arithmetic: it is the term with $\#A$ many Ss applied to $\underline{o}$. As this is already part of our language of arithmetic, we have naming without any additions at all: $T\langle A \rangle$—that is, $T(\underline{\#A})$—can serve as the claim that A is true. This is, in the first place, a claim about a *number*—$\#A$—but it can stand in for a claim about A because of the connection between A and $\#A$.

Moreover, and this is where something like self-reference shows up, it is possible to show that, for any formula $A(x)$ with one variable free, there is a sentence D provably equivalent to $A(\langle D \rangle)$. (This is called the *diagonal lemma*.) To construct a Liar sentence, consider the formula $\neg Tx$, and apply the diagonal lemma to it. This yields a sentence λ provably equivalent to $\neg T\langle \lambda \rangle$.

This is not exactly self-reference, for two reasons; but it is close enough. First, λ is not the same sentence as $\neg T\langle \lambda \rangle$; it is only equivalent to it. But equivalence is a tight connection, and this slippage usually does not much matter.[7] Second, $\neg T\langle\lambda\rangle$ does not refer to the sentence λ at all, but only to the number #λ associated with it. But so long as T picks out the property of numbers corresponding to truth of the sentences they are associated with, it is enough to refer to #λ.

Although this approach is more complicated and indirect than the other approaches we consider, it does have notable upsides. One is how automatic it is. Once we've got arithmetic (which we may well want independently), we can follow this approach to talk about our language itself, without any extra provisions or fuss.

Another advantage is witnessed by the functions $\wedge$, $\vee$, etc. These allow us not just to refer to formulas one by one, but also to theorize about structural relations between them: about the relations between conjunctions and their conjuncts, for example. (See §4.3.)

Finally, especially in a classical setting, starting with arithmetic gives some technical advantages. Though they go beyond the scope of this book, one can compute the strength of various extensions of arithmetic in various ways. If we build a theory of truth on top of arithmetic, we can then compare its strength to some of these well-known theories, and so get a kind of measure of our results.

But these advantages come with corresponding disadvantages. While arithmetic is well-understood in traditional classical or intuitionist settings, the precise details are still unclear in a variety of nonclassical settings. So, while fully classical approaches can take arithmetic for granted, nonclassical approaches often cannot. As redoing arithmetic in a nonclassical setting is a tall order in its own right (e.g., Mortensen, 1995; Restall, 1994), nonclassical approaches

---

[7] There are also ways to make this connection stronger, for cases where it does matter. See for example (Heck, 2007).

to paradox often prefer to get directly to the paradoxes, and so take one of the other strategies previously discussed, which are less sensitive to the details of the underlying logic.

The second potential disadvantage to this approach is the well-known *incompleteness* of arithmetic. It is possible to give complete proof systems for a variety of approaches to paradox, but including all of the arithmetic blocks this. At least it does in a classical setting; the jury is still out for some nonclassical ones. (See Priest (1979, 2003).) This is only a disadvantage for some purposes: complete proof systems are only worth what they're worth, after all. But if completeness is a goal, the other approaches to naming can work with it; arithmetic cannot.

4.3 Compositional principles

In addition to capture and release, there are also natural *compositional principles* governing the truth predicate that we ought to consider. These are the formal analogues of such truisms as "A conjunction is true iff its conjuncts are", "A negation is true iff its negatum isn't true", and so on. Clearly, these can only be formulated in a language with enough resources to talk about one sentence's being the conjunction of two others, and so on. Of our previous three approaches to naming, then, only the arithmetic method allows for formulation and discussion of these principles.[8] Formalized, these claims look like

---

[8] Any system that features a "transparent truth predicate" (i.e., a predicate T such that $T\langle A \rangle$ and A are intersubstitutable in the system) and also has $A \leftrightarrow A$ as a theorem, for some biconditional $\leftrightarrow$, will include things *resembling* instances of such principles: for any conjunction $A \wedge B$, for example, $T\langle A \wedge B \rangle \leftrightarrow (T\langle A \rangle \wedge T\langle B \rangle)$ will be a theorem. But this is well short of the principles we are considering: although $A \wedge B$ is in fact the conjunction of A with B, there is nothing *in that sentence* that records this. It is something we know, outside the system. The compositional principles we are concerned with, on the other hand, operate *inside* the system.

$$\forall x \forall y (\texttt{sent}(x \mathbin{\underset{\cdot}{\wedge}} y) \rightarrow (T(x \mathbin{\underset{\cdot}{\wedge}} y) \leftrightarrow (Tx \wedge Ty)))$$

and so on.

We have here restricted the principle to (closed) sentences, and stuck to truth rather than satisfaction. Given a satisfaction predicate, it would be natural to want stronger principles that apply to all formulas, to record truisms like "a satisfies a conjunction of formulas iff it satisfies each of the conjuncts". Moreover, stating appropriate compositional principles even just for truth still requires thinking in terms of satisfaction and formulas, when it comes to the case of the quantifiers. We will not discuss these principles much in the rest of this discussion, but we again record our preference for approaches that can deliver these compositional principles. (Because of the tight tie between syntax and arithmetic, we discuss some approaches for which it is unknown whether they are or are not compatible with these principles—again, nonclassical arithmetic is full of open questions. But we skip over approaches that are known to be incompatible with the compositional principles.)

4.4 Consequence relations

In Chapter 5, we will encounter a number of different logics, presented in a few different ways. The core feature of a logic is its *consequence relation*, which tells you what follows from what. There are several ways to specify consequence relations, but they group into two families: some tell you how the truth of sentences is preserved, and some tell you how to construct proofs.

When we look at the first family, the intuitive idea is that B follows logically from A, written $A \models B$, if it is impossible for A to be true but B not true. We capture this by working with a set of "cases" (in the terminology of Beall and Restall (2006)). $A \models B$ iff in every case in which A is true, B is also true.

When we talk about "cases", formally we use models. A model will consist of a pair $\langle D, I \rangle$, where D is a domain of individuals, and I assigns values to the basic vocabulary of the language, like terms and predicates. A logic is substantially determined by a set of models, which give us the "cases". But something more is needed: we need to say what it is for something to be true in a case, to be able to apply the Beall–Restall definition.

We defined a model in terms of how it interprets the basic vocabulary of a language, but something needs to determine how complex sentences are evaluated in the model. For example, we might say that a conjunction is true in the model iff both of its conjuncts are. A total strategy for evaluating complex sentences is called a *valuation scheme*. A consequence relation is determined by the combination of a space of models and a valuation scheme. In many discussions, we identify logics with these consequence relations.

Many different consequence relations can be defined in this way. In fact, *every* consequence relation meeting a few quite general conditions can be presented as preserving truth-in-a-case in this way.[9]

Another way to think about consequence is in terms of *proofs*. On this way of thinking, B is a consequence of A if there is a proof of B from A.

---

[9] The conditions are sometimes called reflexivity, monotonicity, and transitivity—but beware! Neither "reflexivity" nor "transitivity", when applied to consequence relations, means exactly what it usually means as a property of a binary relation. For discussion of the general presentation of these consequence relations as preserving truth-in-a-case, see Dunn and Hardegree (2001); Humberstone (2012). (Cases in this quite general setting are often called "valuations".)

If you took a first logic course, you are probably familiar with some system for writing formal proofs. It may have involved axioms and rules of inference, and perhaps some mechanism for keeping track of premises. For much of our discussion, especially when it comes to classical logic, you can think of any proof system you like. All that is important is the idea of a proof showing that some sentence B follows from some sentence A, or some set of sentences Γ. We often write this $\Gamma \vdash B$.[10]

In some places, especially in Chapter 7, we will need to be more careful about how a particular proof system works. When this is important, we will introduce the necessary ideas.

Note that whether a consequence relation is presented by models or by proofs is not a fundamental fact about the consequence relation itself: we often have a choice of which way to present a particular consequence relation, and it can be the very same relation being presented in different ways. Similarly, the very same consequence relation can be determined by two different model-space/valuation-scheme combinations, or by two different proof systems. The choice is not always completely arbitrary—sometimes one presentation or another is easier to work with, or reveals some features of philosophical importance, or allows for connections to other consequence relations or mathematical structures—but there is often a certain amount of freedom in how a consequence relation is presented. Here, we will aim to choose the presentations of the consequence relations we consider that we think best capture the features of immediate interest.

---

[10] Note that $\vdash$ is overloaded: sometimes it is a generic notation for any kind of entailment, and sometimes it indicates a specific proof-based idea of entailment. Both uses are standard.

CHAPTER FIVE

Nonclassical Logic
Unrestricted Capture–Release

One of the leading ideas for how to resolve the Liar paradox is that it shows us something about which logic to adopt. The main idea is that the principles of capture and release are the fundamental—indeed, essential—principles governing truth, and should not be given up.[1] Instead, to avoid a logical disaster of the kind we reviewed in §3.1, some other ingredient of the disaster must go. But the only other ingredients were purely logical. This is how we can draw conclusions about logic, as a whole, from paradoxes like the Liar.

This chapter will explore some approaches that undermine the paradoxical argument by appealing to a so-called nonclassical logic. A rough and ready understanding of the difference between classical and nonclassical logics is familiar enough, but a very precise understanding of the difference is not easy to come by. This is because there are a number of incompatible understandings of "classical logic" that are or have been in currency. For example, as they were first studied and understood (for example in Lewis and Langford (1959)), modal logics were taken to be alternatives

---

[1] In what sense "essential"? In what sense "shouldn't be given up"? These are questions for the philosophy of truth—for different philosophical conceptions of truth—to answer. We briefly return to this issue in footnote 7.

to classical logic; nowadays they are more commonly considered *extensions* of classical logic, retaining what was there but adding additional vocabulary. Relevant logics too can and have been viewed in both ways, although they are still more typically taken to be nonclassical than classical.[2] Supervaluationist logics, too, are classical on some understandings (Keefe, 2000) but not others (Hyde, 1997; Williamson, 1994). At issue is exactly which properties of one or more standard presentations are necessary for being classical, and which properties are merely incidental to those presentations. It does not seem that there is a unique best answer to this question; different distinctions are important for different purposes.

In Chapter 7, such worries about the line(s) between classical and nonclassical logic become a bit more pressing, and we will find reason to distinguish two understandings of "classical logic." But for this chapter we don't need worry too much: a rough and ready understanding suffices. All the logics to be considered in this chapter allow for the paradoxical derivations of §3.1 to fail, and all allow for capture and release to apply in full generality. As a result, all allow for the failure of some logical "law" or other mentioned in §3.1.3.2. For now, anyway, we take this to be sufficient for nonclassicality.

One important way to motivate nonclassical solutions is to appeal to a form of *deflationism* about truth.[3] Such views take something akin to the T-schema to be the defining characteristic of truth, and so not open to modification, on pain of not talking about

---

[2] For discussion of how to see relevant logics as extensions of classical logic, see Meyer and Routley (1973, 1974).

[3] This is one way the philosophy of truth—in the form of a particular philosophical conception of the nature of truth (or lack thereof)—might be seen to bear on formal theories of truth.

truth at all (e.g., Armour-Garb and Beall, 2001, 2003). Most strictly, so-called transparency or "see-through" or "pure disquotational" conceptions of truth (e.g., Beall, 2005, 2009; Field, 1994, 2008) take the defining property of truth to be the *intersubstitutability* of A and $T\langle A \rangle$ in all non-opaque contexts (i.e., in too-simplistic terms, contexts in which the substitution of identities doesn't fail). This makes capture and release, in unrestricted form applying to all sentences of a language, a requirement for truth (at least if entailment is reflexive; that is, if $A \vdash A$).[4]

Holding capture and release fixed, and applying it to all sentences without restriction, threatens to yield triviality, if the logical "laws" of §3.1.3.2 hold and if paradoxical sentences are formulable. But just failing some of these laws is not enough; the derivations we've exhibited are just some of infinitely many routes to triviality via paradox. Blocking one, or a few particular, derivations is no guarantee of overall safety. This has motivated detailed development of nonclassical theories of truth. Many of these theories share a common core: the construction of Kripke (1975). As such, we first outline this common core, before discussing some ways in which it has been developed.

5.1 Kleene–Kripke models

This section briefly sketches the kind of structure we call *Kleene–Kripke models*, a kind of three-valued model widely used in the study of transparent truth. First, we explore so-called *strong Kleene models*, three-valued models that pay no special attention to truth.

---

[4] Two of us have argued for a close connection between general views on the nature of truth and available avenues for resolving the paradox (Beall and Glanzberg, 2008). The third is not convinced. (Discussion in Scharp (2013, Ch. 1) is also relevant.)

Then we see how to extend them via the construction described in Kripke (1975), to Kleene–Kripke models, which are particularly suited for exploring a transparent truth predicate.

5.1.1 Strong Kleene models

A strong Kleene model is a pair $\langle D, I \rangle$ of a domain D and an interpretation I. The domain is a set; it can contain whatever you like, although it is usually assumed to be nonempty. The interpretation function assigns values of various sorts to pieces of vocabulary: terms are assigned members of the domain, sentences are assigned values, and n-ary predicates are assigned functions from D^n to values. Strong Kleene models are three-valued; the values assigned to sentences are drawn from $\{1, \frac{1}{2}, 0\}$. (Really all that matters about this set of values is that it has three members, but using these numbers allows for concise statements of some important relations between them.)

Values 1 and 0 in strong Kleene models behave much as they do in two-valued classical models. As a heuristic, when a model assigns 1 (0) to a sentence, you can think of the sentence as being true in the model (false in the model), although you should remember that there is a big difference between being true in a model and being true! (More discussion of this in §5.4.3.) The value $\frac{1}{2}$, on the other hand, is genuinely new, and as it is distinct from 0 and 1, it is often glossed as representing "neither true nor false." But this can be seriously misleading, if not flat-out question-begging: no particular way of thinking of this value is part of the common core we are outlining here. Different philosophical approaches understand these values (particularly $\frac{1}{2}$) in different ways.

Just as in the classical case, values for complex sentences can be calculated from the values of their components. For any strong

Kleene model $\langle D, I \rangle$, and any pair of sentences A, B, we have the following requirements:

- $I(A \wedge B) = \min(I(A), I(B))$
- $I(A \vee B) = \max(I(A), I(B))$
- $I(\neg A) = 1 - I(A)$

This preserves all the usual classical truth-functions on 1 and 0, and extends them to cover combinations involving the new value in a particularly intuitive way. It also preserves familiar De Morgan connections between $\neg$, $\vee$, and $\wedge$; for example, you can use these requirements to show that $I(\neg(A \wedge B))$ is always (in all such models) identical to $I(\neg A \vee \neg B)$. The material conditional $A \supset B$ can be defined as $\neg A \vee B$ as usual, so that we have

$$I(A \supset B) = \max(1 - I(A), I(B)).$$

Also, just as in the classical case, values for quantified sentences can be calculated from the values of their instances; this can be handled objectually or substitutionally, to taste. However it is handled though, $I(\forall x A(x))$ is the minimum value taken by the instances of $A(x)$, and $I(\exists x A(x))$ is the maximum such value. Again, this yields the usual classical values when all instances receive classical values. Also, quantifiers too turn out to obey some usual equivalences; for example, $I(\forall x \neg A(x)) = I(\neg \exists x A(x))$.

One more thing to note before we move on: usual two-valued classical models are a special kind of strong Kleene model. As long as no predicate in a strong Kleene model assigns $\frac{1}{2}$ to any tuple from the domain, the model will be a classical model of the ordinary sort. So, if we discover anything about all strong Kleene models of a certain type, it will hold as well of all classical models of that type. We stop there; for more thorough presentations, see Beall (2010); Beall and van Fraassen (2003); Priest (2008).

5.1.2 Fixed points

Suppose we have a strong Kleene model $\langle D, I \rangle$ for a language $\mathcal{L}$ that does not include a truth predicate, and we want to expand it to a model $\langle D, I' \rangle$ for an expanded language $\mathcal{L}^+$ that does include a truth predicate. Suppose furthermore that we insist this truth predicate obey full capture and release. Of course, we will have to assume our language has an appropriate way to name sentences, as we discussed in Chapter 4. Thus, let us assume that $\mathcal{L}$ contains a term $\langle A \rangle$ for every sentence of $\mathcal{L}^+$.[5]

What Kripke (1975) shows is that there is always a way to build an interpretation $\langle D, I' \rangle$ that gives us full capture and release. The basic idea is simple. On every bit of language in $\mathcal{L}$, I' is just the same as I. The only difference is that I' assigns an appropriate value to the predicate T as well. (I, remember, doesn't assign anything at all to T.) Since T is a one-place predicate, it needs to be assigned some function t from members of the domain to values. To ensure transparency, we need to make sure that $t(A) = I'(A)$, for every $A \in \mathcal{L}^+$. That way, it will hold that $I'(T\langle A \rangle) = I'(A)$. If there is such a function, then I' can assign it to T, and we have our target model.

The target model will not only assign the same value to A and $T\langle A \rangle$; it will also assign the same value to any sentences that result from each other by swapping As for $T\langle A \rangle$s or vice versa. This is because all the connectives and quantifiers in play take values that depend only on the values of their inputs. Since A and $T\langle A \rangle$ have the same value, they will result in the same value. This is what will suffice for full transparency.

---

[5] That is, we assume that $I(\langle A \rangle) = A$ for every such sentence. To handle satisfaction as well as truth, a few more assumptions are needed; and the idea works for more than just strong Kleene models. We stay light here on the details of the whole construction, though. For an accessible overview, see Soames (1999). For a more mathematically rich exposition, see McGee (1991).

First, though, it must be shown that there is such a function. (There always is. In fact, there are usually many such functions!) Kripke shows this via a construction that goes through a number of candidate functions t_n before it finds one that will do. Here's how it works. For each such t_n, let I_n be the interpretation that is just like I except that it assigns t_n to T. Let t_0 be the function that sends everything to $\frac{1}{2}$. Now, when n is a successor ordinal, so $n = m + 1$ for some m, then let t_n be just like t_m except that it assigns $I_m(A)$ to A, for all $A \in \mathcal{L}^+$. When n is a limit ordinal, let $t_n(A) = 0$ if there is some $m < n$ such that $t_m(A) = 0$, let $t_n(A) = 1$ if there is some $m < n$ such that $t_m(A) = 1$, and let $t_n(A) = \frac{1}{2}$ otherwise.

It takes a bit of doing to show that these t_n functions are well-defined at limit stages; but they are. Moreover, they reach a *fixed point*: there is some t_k such that $t_k = t_{k+1}$. (In fact, for such a t_k, we have $t_k = t_n$ for all $n \geq k$.) Since we defined t_{k+1} so that $t_{k+1}(A) = I_k(A)$ for all $A \in \mathcal{L}^+$, it follows that $t_k(A) = I_k(A)$ for all such A; let $I' = I_k$, and we have the desired model: one that adds a transparent truth predicate to our original strong Kleene model, without changing anything else.

This construction doesn't have to start at the particular t_0 mentioned previously; many other possible choices for t_0 will work as well.[6] Different choices will give different results, but all the workable ones will have the crucial features mentioned: the resulting model will not change anything in the original model, and it will feature a fully transparent truth predicate. The t_0 we started at gives what is often called the *minimal fixed point*; other choices yield other fixed points. We will call the models resulting from this construction *Kleene–Kripke models*, or *KK models*.

---

[6] Not all choices, though. What's needed is that whenever $t_0(A) = 1$ or 0, then $I_0(A) = t_0(A)$. Kremer (1988) calls these choices 'fixable', and that seems like a fine name.

Note that the original model can be fully classical, and it is still covered by this construction, since two-valued classical models are just a kind of strong Kleene–Kripke model. This includes models containing enough arithmetic to give a full theory of the syntax of $\mathcal{L}^+$, or models containing such syntax directly. The KK model that results from the construction will not be a classical model of the usual sort, though, if anything like a Liar sentence is formulable in $\mathcal{L}^+$.

Consider, as usual, a Liar sentence λ such that λ is equivalent to $\neg T\langle\lambda\rangle$. On any KK model $\langle D, I \rangle$, we know $I(\neg T\langle\lambda\rangle) = 1 - I(T\langle\lambda\rangle)$, and on any KK model that respects the connection between λ and $\langle\lambda\rangle$, we know $I(T\langle\lambda\rangle) = I(\lambda)$. It follows that $I(\neg T\langle\lambda\rangle) = 1 - I(\lambda)$; but $\neg T\langle\lambda\rangle$ is λ, so $I(\lambda) = 1 - I(\lambda)$. The only possibility then, is that $I(\lambda) = \frac{1}{2}$. The same can be shown of other paradoxical sentences; on all KK models, paradoxical sentences take the value $\frac{1}{2}$. (Indeed, Kripke (1975) offers this as a definition of "paradoxical.")

5.2 Consequence

Given these models, there are a number of different ways to define consequence. This section mainly discusses two of the best-known options; these options yield logics we will call K3TT and LPTT, for "K3 with Transparent Truth" and "LP with Transparent Truth."[7] At the end of the section, however, we briefly mention two other options that occur in the literature for understanding consequence in terms of KK models, as well as an option that uses a slightly more general kind of model.

[7] "K3" and "LP" are standard names for the T-free parts of these logics. K3 is so called for Kleene and its three-valued presentation (Kleene, 1952). "LP" comes from "Logic of Paradox"; it was given this name by Priest (1979), although the logic itself

All these logics feature a transparent truth predicate. Since on any KK model, swapping As for $T\langle A\rangle$s and vice versa does not affect the value of any sentence, any way of defining consequence that depends only on the values assigned to sentences will be insensitive to such a swap—and all our potential ways of defining consequence are like this.

To define a notion of consequence model-theoretically, all it takes is to say what it is for a model to be a *countermodel* to an argument. Given this, validity can be defined as absence of countermodel: an argument is valid iff no model is a countermodel to it. Both K3TT and LPTT use the idea of *designated values* to specify their countermodels. In each case, a countermodel to an argument is a *KK* model that assigns a designated value to each premise and does not assign a designated value to any conclusion.[8] The difference between K3TT and LPTT is just in which values count as designated.

5.2.1 A paracomplete logic: K3TT

K3TT is the logic that results from taking 1 to be the sole designated value. That is, an argument is K3TT-invalid iff there is a *KK* model that assigns 1 to every premise of the argument and does not assign 1 to any of its conclusions; it is K3TT-valid otherwise. We will write $\Gamma \vDash_{K3TT} \Delta$ to say that the argument from Γ to Δ is K3TT-valid.

was advanced by Asenjo earlier (Asenjo, 1966; Asenjo and Tamburino, 1975) as a way of treating paradoxical or "antinomic" sentences as "gluts"—the idea being that such gluts (or "antinomic sentences") should not only be accepted in our true theories, but seen as important discoveries for mathematics. For discussion of the relation between (first-order) LP and what is called (first-order) LA (for "logic of antinomies," using the Asenjo and Asenjo-Tamburino terminology of "antinomy"), see Beall *et al.* (2014). (Asenjo seemed to be chiefly interested in *necessary gluts* or *essential gluts,* for which the term "antinomy" is reserved in Beall *et al.* (2014). Priest (1979) and other glut theorists were interested in "contingent gluts" and not just antinomies (so understood).

[8] This is for multiple-conclusion validity; single-conclusion validity is a special case.

K3TT gives us a notion of consequence that respects many classical validities. For example, the De Morgan equivalences are K3TT-valid, and so are quantifier dualities, as can be seen from the discussion of *KK* models. Here are a few more examples:

Adjunction: $A, B \vDash_{K3TT} A \wedge B$
Abjunction: $A \vee B \vDash_{K3TT} A, B$
⊃-modus-ponens: $A, A \supset B \vDash_{K3TT} B$
Double negation: $A \vDash_{K3TT} \neg\neg A$ and $\neg\neg A \vDash_{K3TT} A$
Explosion (ECQ): $A, \neg A \vDash_{K3TT} B$ (or $A, \neg A \vDash_{K3TT}$)

K3TT validity is nonclassical, however. Importantly, the law of excluded middle (LEM) is not a theorem: $\nvDash_{K3TT} A \vee \neg A$. In fact, K3TT has no theorems at all! To see this, consider a KK model that assigns every sentence the value $\frac{1}{2}$. (You can check to see that there is such a *KK* model.) This model is a countermodel to any alleged theorem, since it takes all sentences to an undesignated value.

It's not just that some instances of LEM *can* fail in K3TT, however. According to *paracomplete* theories of paradox, this is exactly where the argument of §3.1.3.3 fails: in step 4, where it appeals to $T\langle\lambda\rangle \vee \neg T\langle\lambda\rangle$, an instance of LEM. Recall that λ must take the value $\frac{1}{2}$ on *KK* models; then $T\langle\lambda\rangle \vee \neg T\langle\lambda\rangle$ must take the value $\frac{1}{2}$ as well. As a result, we cannot appeal to LEM in this way; this is the paracomplete diagnosis.[9]

5.2.2 *A paraconsistent logic: LPTT*

LPTT is the logic that results from taking 1 and $\frac{1}{2}$ both to be designated values, and leaving 0 as the sole undesignated value. That is, an argument is LPTT-invalid iff there is a KK model that assigns 0 to every conclusion of the argument and does not assign

---

[9] The classic presentation of K3TT is Kripke (1975) himself. For more on K3 in a non-classical setting, see Beall and van Fraassen (2003); Priest (2008).

o to any of its premises; it is LPTT-valid otherwise. We will write $\Gamma \vDash_{LPTT} \Delta$ to say that the argument from Γ to Δ is LPTT-valid.[10]

LPTT too gives us a notion of consequence that respects many classical validities. For example, the De Morgan equivalences are LPTT-valid, and so are quantifier dualities, as can be seen from the discussion of KK models. Here are a few more examples:

Adjunction: $A, B \vDash_{LPTT} A \wedge B$
Abjunction: $A \vee B \vDash_{LPTT} A, B$
⊃-identity: $\vDash_{LPTT} A \supset A$
Double negation: $A \vDash_{LPTT} \neg\neg A$ and $\neg\neg A \vDash_{LPTT} A$
LEM: $B \vDash_{LPTT} A \vee \neg A$ (or $\vDash_{LPTT} A \vee \neg A$)

LPTT validity is also nonclassical, however. Importantly, explosion is not LPTT-valid: $A, \neg A \nvDash_{LPTT} B$, and $A \wedge \neg A \nvDash_{LP} B$. It's not just that some instances of explosion *can* fail in LPTT, however. According to *paraconsistent* theories of paradox, this is exactly where the argument of §3.1.3.3 fails: at the very last step, where it moves from $T\langle\lambda\rangle \wedge \neg T\langle\lambda\rangle$ to an arbitrary B. Recall that λ must take the value $\frac{1}{2}$ on KK models; then $T\langle\lambda\rangle \wedge \neg T\langle\lambda\rangle$ must take the value $\frac{1}{2}$ as well. B, though, might have any value, since it is arbitrary. If it has value o on a *KK* model, then that model is a countermodel to the last step.

To stop only here commits the advocate of such an approach to a contradiction: $T\langle\lambda\rangle \wedge \neg T\langle\lambda\rangle$. According to this approach, then, some contradictions are true; it is thus a so-called *glutty* or *dialetheic* approach.[11]

---

[10] Note that $\Gamma \vDash_{LPTT} \Delta$ iff $\neg\Delta \vDash_{K_3TT} \neg\Gamma$, where $\neg\Gamma = \{\neg\gamma : \gamma \in \Gamma\}$, and similarly for $\neg\Delta$.

[11] For further discussion of glutty (or 'glut-theoretic') or dialetheic (sometimes 'dialethic') approaches, see Asenjo (1966); Beall (2009); Priest (2006a,b). The term 'glutty' is from Fine (1974); 'dialetheic', from Priest and Routley (1989). There is an important and sometimes-overlooked distinction between *paraconsistency* and

5.2.3 Neither and both

Sometimes, paracomplete and glutty views are contrasted by saying that paracomplete views take paradoxical sentences to be neither true nor false, while glutty views take paradoxical sentences to be both true and false. The (bad) idea is that K3TT partisans take the value $\frac{1}{2}$ to stand for "neither true nor false" while LPTT partisans take it to stand for "both true and false." Thus, in assigning λ the value $\frac{1}{2}$, K3TT is understood to say that it is neither true nor false; while in assigning λ the value $\frac{1}{2}$, LPTT is understood to say that it is both true and false. But this is simply wrong; it does not accurately represent what these theories say. It is worth taking a moment to see why this is so.

Consider the claim that the Liar is neither true nor false. This claim can be formalized in our object language as: $\neg(T\langle\lambda\rangle \vee T\langle\neg\lambda\rangle)$. By a De Morgan equivalence, this claim is equivalent to $\neg T\langle\lambda\rangle \wedge \neg T\langle\neg\lambda\rangle$. Reordering the conjuncts and appealing to transparency shows that the claim is equivalent to $\neg\neg T\langle\lambda\rangle \wedge T\langle\neg\lambda\rangle$. Finally, appeal to a double-negation equivalence shows that the claim is equivalent to $T\langle\lambda\rangle \wedge T\langle\neg\lambda\rangle$—the claim that the Liar is

---

glut theory. To adopt a paraconsistent view is to reject the validity of explosion, while to adopt a glutty view is to accept some contradiction—some *glut* (of truth and falsity). Given some usual (but not uncontroversial; see Chapter 7) assumptions, glut theorists ought to go for paraconsistency; but there are reasons other than glut theory to adopt a paraconsistent logic (for example, those presented in Anderson and Belnap (1975); Routley *et al.* (1982)).

When it comes to paradox, though, the distinction doesn't much matter: there seems to be no way to appeal to paraconsistency to block the derivation in §3.1.3.3 without also accepting gluts. One could (and should!) draw the corresponding distinction between *paracompleteness* and *gap theory* or *analetheism*, but for whatever reason it is less usual to insist on the distinction. See Burgess and Burgess (2011); Maudlin (2004); Parsons (1984) for ideas around analetheism (and see Beall and Ripley (2004) for a different though related use of the term).

both true and false. All of this reasoning goes through as is in both K_3 and LP, and so in K_3TT and LPTT as well.

Paracomplete and paraconsistent views alike—at least, those committed to the logics we discuss in this chapter—thus agree that the claim that the Liar is neither true nor false is *equivalent* to the claim that it is both true and false. The claims must stand or fall together, on these views. It certainly is not the case, then, that one view accepts the "neither" claim while the other accepts the "both" claim instead. Rather, paracomplete theorists reject both these claims, while glut theorists accept them both. This is related to some prima facie difficulties for these approaches, which we will discuss in §5.4.2.

5.2.4 *Some alternatives*

Here, we quickly mention two other ways to define consequence from *KK* models. Neither of these uses a notion of designated value; they work in other ways. We also mention an additional related approach that uses more general models.

The logic FDRMTT is defined as follows:[12] a *KK* model is an FDRMTT countermodel to an argument iff the lowest value it assigns to any premise is higher than the highest value it assigns to any conclusion. Another way to look at this: all K_3TT countermodels to an argument are FDRMTT countermodels to that argument, and so are all LPTT countermodels, and nothing else is an FDRMTT countermodel. As a result, the arguments that are FDRMTT-valid are exactly the arguments that are both

---

[12] The logic appears to have no standard name. We call it FDRMTT: the "TT" is for "Transparent Truth" as usual, while the "FDRM" stands for "First Degree RM," by analogy with the more well-known FDE, or First-Degree E; FDRM stands in the same relation to the logic RM as FDE does to the logic E. Both RM and E are discussed in Anderson and Belnap (1975).

K3TT-valid and LPTT-valid. From this point of view, the argument of §3.1.3.3 is thus doubly invalid: Once in its use of LEM, and again in its use of explosion. We will not discuss this approach further here; it is explored in Halbach and Horsten (2006); Kremer (1988).

The logic STTT is defined as follows:[13] a KK model is an STTT countermodel to an argument iff it assigns 1 to every premise of the argument and 0 to every conclusion of the argument. This is a more difficult condition to meet than any of the other conditions we've looked at; as a result, more arguments are STTT-valid than are K3TT-valid, LPTT-valid, or FDRMTT-valid. STTT is nonclassical by the rough-and-ready lights of this chapter, as it fails Closure, but it turns out to be classical on some other precisifications of the idea. We will return to it—and this distinction—in Chapter 7, where we will consider STTT in more detail.

Note that all the ways of defining consequence we've seen so far—preserving value 1 (K3), preserving nonzero value (LP), not lowering in value (FDRM), not going from 1 to 0 (ST)—reduce to the familiar classical notion on two-valued models. K3, LP, FDRM, and ST thus are all different ways to generalize classical consequence to the richer space of strong Kleene models.[14]

Finally, there is the logic FDETT.[15] This logic is not based on KK models, but on related four-valued models treated in a corresponding way. Intuitively, these four-valued models have one value that behaves the way $\frac{1}{2}$ does in K3TT (and so is not designated), and a different value that behaves the way $\frac{1}{2}$ does

[13] The name is for "Strict-Tolerant"; it is discussed in Cobreros *et al.* (2013); Ripley (2012, 2013).

[14] You could also consider "not going from non-zero to non-one." This notion of consequence on strong Kleene models, called TS in Cobreros *et al.* (2013); Ripley (2012), is empty in the present vocabulary: no argument at all is TS-valid, not even the argument from p to p. Nonetheless, the idea still has some uses in this area; for one, see Meadows (2014).

[15] Recall footnote 12.

in LPTT (and so is designated). The resulting logic is close to FDRMTT, but slightly weaker;[16] its extensions are explored by Brady (1989a); Dunn (1969); Gupta and Belnap (1993); Visser (1984); Woodruff (1984); Yablo (1993a), and others.

For the remainder of this chapter, we focus on K3TT and LPTT, but much of what we say can be applied as well to at least some of these other approaches.

5.3 Extra conditionals

Often, those who defend a nonclassical theory of truth do not stop at logics like K3TT or LPTT, but instead extend those logics with an extra conditional connective. For example, Priest (2006b) extends a close relative of LPTT in this way, Brady (2006) extends FDETT in this way, Field (2008) extends K3TT in this way, and Beall (2009) extends LPTT in this way. The purpose of this section is to explain why this is such a common approach, and sketch some constraints that those who take this approach must face. In this section, we will continue to use the symbols $\supset$ and $\equiv$ for the material conditional and biconditional, respectively; we will use $\rightarrow$ and $\leftrightarrow$ ambiguously, sometimes to cover any old conditional/biconditional connective, and sometimes for particular extra conditionals/biconditionals used by various theorists. (In every case, we assume that $A \leftrightarrow B$ abbreviates $(A \rightarrow B) \wedge (B \rightarrow A)$.)

5.3.1 *Why an extra conditional?*

There are a few reasons why K3TT and LPTT (and their relatives) are often extended with an extra conditional connective. First, a

---

[16] The most notable difference: $A \wedge \neg A \vDash_{FDRMTT} B \vee \neg B$, but $A \wedge \neg A \nvDash_{FDETT} B \vee \neg B$.

number of principles often taken to be important for conditionals simply do not hold of the material conditional in K3TT or LPTT. For example, $\not\vdash_{K3TT} A \supset A$, and $A, A \supset B \not\vdash_{LPTT} B$. To the extent that we want to model our ordinary understanding of conditionals, it does not look like $\supset$ is up to the job.[17] Usually, the extra conditional is such that $\vdash A \to A$ and $A, A \to B \vdash B$ in the resulting logic; these principles are sometimes called "$\to$-identity" and "$\to$-detachment."

Second, some conditional or other is intimately involved in the T-schema: $A \leftrightarrow T\langle A\rangle$. But if that conditional is material, then the T-scheme is not a theorem of K3TT, since nothing at all is. Moreover, instances of the material T-schema that involve paradoxical sentences are not even *satisfiable* in K3TT; they cannot receive a designated value. To the extent that the unrestricted T-schema is an important part of a theory of truth, K3TT-based approaches need to find some other conditional connective to appear in it. We might find the T-schema important, for instance, since we might want to report (or *make explicit*, in the sense of Brandom (1994)) in our language the central entailment properties of truth, like capture and release. Without the T-schema, we do not have a way to do this.

It is sometimes thought that LPTT-based approaches face a similar difficulty here, since, although they validate the unrestricted material T-schema, they do not validate modus ponens on it, since they do not validate material modus ponens in general. Something like this worry is expressed, for example, in Beall (2009, p. 26). But, at least expressed like this, this is an error. While material modus ponens is not in general valid in LPTT, those instances of it in which

---

[17] Of course, there are compelling reasons to think that $\supset$ is not up to this job even in a classical setting (e.g., Kratzer, 1979; Routley *et al.*, 1982), but the problems are all the worse in K3TT and LPTT.

an instance of the T-schema provides the conditional in question *are* all valid. That is, $A, A \equiv T\langle A \rangle \vDash_{LPTT} T\langle A \rangle$, and $T\langle A \rangle, A \equiv T\langle A \rangle \vDash_{LPTT} A$; these validities hold for any A.

An advocate of LPTT might still worry that, while these instances of material modus ponens are all valid, they are not valid *for the right reasons*: the conditional itself is idle in these validities, since $A \vDash_{LPTT} T\langle A \rangle$ and $T\langle A \rangle \vDash_{LPTT} A$ already, without any extra conditional premises. This, we think, is the best way to press this worry, although how to make it precise, and whether it is worth pressing, is a tricky issue we leave to one side. Suffice to say it has been part of the motivation for adding an additional conditional to LPTT.[18]

5.3.2 *Some constraints*

Adding such an extra conditional is not without its pitfalls, however. Most worrisome is the risk of Curry paradox formulated with the new conditional. Pick any sentence B, and let κ be the sentence $T\langle \kappa \rangle \to B$. Now we can reason as follows:

1.	$\kappa \to \kappa$	$[\to\text{-identity}]$
2.	$\kappa \to (T\langle \kappa \rangle \to B)$	[restatement of 1]
3.	$T\langle \kappa \rangle \to (T\langle \kappa \rangle \to B)$	[2, transparency]
4.	$T\langle \kappa \rangle \to B$	$[3, \to\text{-contraction}]$
5.	κ	[restatement of 4]
6.	$T\langle \kappa \rangle$	[5, transparency]
7.	B	$[4, 6, \to\text{-modus ponens}]$

---

[18] Field (2008, p. 369) pushes advocates of LPTT and its relatives to find a conditional for which the *negations* of instances of the T-schema are not theorems. While this would, if accepted as a desideratum, push for adding a non-material conditional to LPTT, no advocate of a glut-theoretic approach accepts this as a desideratum, as far as we know; nor is it clear why they would.

This argument proceeds from identity, via transparency, modus ponens, and $\to$-contraction (the move from $A \to (A \to B)$ to $A \to B$) to yield B. Since B was arbitrary, something must have gone wrong: in the presence of transparent truth, no connective can validate all of identity, modus ponens, and contraction.[19] Moreover, transparency is only a simplification; the argument can be revised to run with just capture and release. The same is true for the identity between κ and $T\langle\kappa\rangle \to B$; equivalence is enough.

The motivations for introducing $\to$ in the first place, though, depend on its validating both identity and modus ponens. It must, then, invalidate contraction. This has struck some as implausible, but defenders of extra-conditional approaches typically just take it as the price of doing business in this area.

There are other constraints that extra conditionals must meet to be suited for various logics. For example, consider adding an extra conditional of this sort to LPTT, and suppose that the conditional validates both weakening ($B \vdash A \to B$) and contraposition ($A \to B \vdash \neg B \to \neg A$), in addition to modus ponens. Then we can use this conditional to derive explosion:

1. A [premise]
2. $\neg A$ [premise]
3. $\neg B \to A$ $[1, \to\text{-weakening}]$
4. $\neg A \to \neg\neg B$ $[3, \to\text{-contraposition}]$
5. $\neg\neg B$ $[2, 4, \to\text{-modus ponens}]$
6. B [5, double negation elimination]

Since an LPTT approach relies crucially on its rejection of explosion to avoid trouble with the Liar paradox, it cannot accept

---

[19] We are here assuming that standard structural rules—particularly transitivity and (structural) contraction—are in force. When we revisit STTT in Chapter 7, we will see that its material conditional does allow for all of identity, modus ponens, and contraction. But STTT is nontransitive.

this. So, no extra conditional added to LPTT can validate all of weakening, contraposition, and modus ponens.

Care is thus required in adding extra conditionals to these logics. Almost always, the extra conditional violates the requirements of the Kripke construction discussed already. If it is to be shown that base models can be extended to models involving transparent truth in these more complicated logics, it requires more complicated proofs. Here, the paradigm is the work of Brady (1971, 1989*b*, 2006, 2014); a still more complicated approach can be found in Field (2008).

The core idea of Brady's constructions in (1971; 1989*b*; 2006) is to interlace two distinct fixed-point constructions. One of them is just like the Kripke construction discussed previously; it holds everything constant except for the extension of the truth predicate, and finds an appropriately transparent choice. The other is novel; it holds everything constant except for conditional sentences, and updates the values assigned to these conditionals, albeit in a way that can break the transparency of the truth predicate. After each update to the conditionals, the full Kripke construction is repeated. Brady shows that this approach will eventually yield a fixed point at which both truth and conditionals behave appropriately. More recently, Brady has developed a variant of this construction involving so-called "metavaluations" (Brady, 2011, 2014).

5.4 Common objections

There are a variety of common objections to K3TT and LPTT-based theories of truth, and some of their relatives. We present three very common objections and point in the direction of common replies.

5.4.1 *Nonclassical logic!*

One objection points to the "departure" from classical logic as dooming the proposal. This is not an easy objection to assess. Though indeed K3TT and LPTT are nonclassical, just how far their nonclassical nature goes is a difficult question. For instance, K3 "collapses" into classical logic if you simply add all instances of LEM.

It is also difficult to assess just how fair this sort of objection is, given other assumptions that might be made. For instance, if you take the Liar to *show* that some instances of LEM cannot hold, then objecting to K3TT on the grounds that it fails to be classical amounts to simply rejecting the paracomplete proposal out of hand. Furthermore, many proponents of paracomplete or paraconsistent approaches take their arguments to show what logic was like all along. Rather than indicating a departure from logic as it was, they take their results to show that logic was always paracomplete or paraconsistent. Transparent truth predicates in particular, can be taken to make vivid just where and how logic is not classical.

At the same time, we note that classical logic has become a default in the eyes of many, not simply out of prejudice or whim, but because of its long and hard-won track record. One illustration of this, as we discuss more presently, is that the standard way of developing either K3TT or LPTT involves using a classical meta-theory, where we do the set theory which builds our Kleene–Kripke models. Classical reasoning is deeply embedded in most of mathematics.[20] Moreover, even those areas of mathematics that

---

[20] So, for instance, Feferman (1984) complains that "sustained ordinary reasoning" cannot be done in K3-like logics. See Beall (2015) for one general direction of reply to these worries.

stray from classical logic frequently work in constructive logics of various sorts; but these tend to be just as vulnerable to the paradoxes as classical logic is, while the nonclassical approaches of this chapter are different.

Proponents of paracomplete or paraconsistent approaches frequently argue that these uses of classical or constructive reasoning can be preserved, even if truth and related concepts reveal a nonclassical nature of logic (Beall 2009, 2013c,a). Other proponents (Priest, 2006b; Routley, 1979; Weber, 2012), have sought to develop non-classical meta-theories. This is an active area of research, and at the time of this book's writing, its success remains unknown.

5.4.2 *Disagreement, claims of paradoxicality, and expressive power*

At least prima facie, advocates of paracomplete and glutty approaches to paradox face a difficulty in expressing disagreement.

Suppose you assert the Liar sentence to a paracompletist. They certainly disagree with you, but how can they express it? Definitely not by asserting the negation of the Liar sentence. That would be going too far; after all, they also disagree with the negation. The whole idea of a paracomplete solution is to reject both the paradoxical sentence and its negation (and so their disjunction as well). But then disagreement had better be expressible without asserting a negation, if it is to be expressible at all.

If you assert the Liar sentence to a glut theorist, on the other hand, they will not disagree with you at all, so this difficulty does not arise. Instead, the difficulty turns up when you assert something they do *not* accept, like "$2 + 2 = 5$." How can they express disagreement with this? Again, asserting the negation will not do the trick, although this time for the opposite reason: it's not going far enough. After all, they would be perfectly happy to assert the negation of the Liar sentence as well, but this should not be taken as *disagreement* with someone who asserts the Liar sentence; the whole idea of a glutty solution is to accept both the paradoxical sentence and its negation. Again, disagreement had better be expressible somehow other than by asserting a negation.

One kind of response to this problem, outlined in Parsons (1984) and taken up in Field (2008); Priest (2006a), is to postulate a negative speech act of denial that cannot be understood in terms of assertion together with negation. Paracompetists and glut theorists alike can then deny things in order to express disagreement of various sorts, while keeping assertions of negations separate.

Although denying something is distinct from asserting its negation, it is commonly supposed that they look (or sound) a lot alike. As a result, it is sometimes a matter requiring some interpretation whether a given paracompletist or glut theorist, in writing (or uttering) a sentence with "not" in it, means to assert the sentence itself or to deny the thing apparently being negated. This, then, explains why a paracompletist might write something like "The Liar is not either true or false"; correctly interpreted, they are not *asserting* that it is *neither*—as we've seen, they cannot— but instead *denying* that it is *either*. Similarly, it explains why a glut theorist might say something like "It's not that everything is true," in an attempt to rule out trivialism; correctly interpreted, they are not *asserting* the sentence—after all, a trivialist would assert it too—but instead *denying* that everything is true.

Paracompletists and glut theorists can thus use this strategy to talk about paradoxicality and nonparadoxicality. While a paracompletist cannot assert that a sentence is neither true nor false to say that it is paradoxical (since they will never assert that of any sentence), they can deny that it is either. And while a glut theorist cannot assert that a sentence is not both true and false to say that it is nonparadoxical (since they will assert that of any sentence you like), they can deny that it is both.

This strategy may have its limits, however. For example, there does not appear to be any way for a paracompletist to appeal to denial to express what we might want to say with "I'll bet you a beer that sentence X is not either true or false," or with "If sentence X is not either true or false, I'll eat my hat." Both of these seem reasonable where sentence X is, say, (DLiar) from §2.5, but the paracompletist who relies only on denial seems to be stuck either insisting that these sentences cannot mean what they seem to, or else admitting that their language is expressively impoverished.

Similarly, there does not appear to be any way for a glut theorist to appeal to denial to express what we might want to say with "I'll bet you a beer that sentence X is consistently true," or with "If sentence X is consistently true, I'll eat my hat." Again, both of these seem reasonable where sentence X is (DLiar), but the glut theorist who relies only on denial seems to be stuck either insisting that these sentences cannot mean what they seem to, or else admitting that their language is expressively impoverished.

The trouble in both cases is that denial is a *speech act*, something a speaker *does*. It cannot be embedded in larger sentential environments, since it's not a piece of syntax. But it seems claims about paradoxicality and nonparadoxicality ought to be embeddable in these larger environments. Relying on denial to express these claims prevents this.

For further discussion of this line of objection, see Ripley (2015); Shapiro (2004). Paracompletists and glut theorists, of course, have worked out responses to these issues. For some of these responses, see Beall (2009, 2013b); Field (2008); Priest (2006a).

5.4.3 *Value 1 and revenge*

A different set of worries comes directly from the model theory of these nonclassical approaches. Suppose we want to include in our language a predicate O to express the notion "takes value 1 in this very model" by restricting our *KK* models so that $I(O\langle A\rangle) = 1$ iff $I(A) = 1$ and $I(O\langle A\rangle) = 0$ otherwise. Then it will turn out that we have a problem on our hands.

Let ζ be the sentence $\neg O\langle\zeta\rangle$. There is no value available for ζ to take: if ζ takes value 1, then $O\langle\zeta\rangle$ must as well, so $\neg O\langle\zeta\rangle$ must take value 0; but if ζ takes either value $\frac{1}{2}$ or value 0, then $O\langle\zeta\rangle$ must take value 0, so $\neg O\langle\zeta\rangle$ must take value 1. Whatever happens, ζ and $\neg O\langle\zeta\rangle$ must take different values, but they are the very same sentence; this is impossible. If we impose the suggested requirement on O, we have imposed inconsistent requirements on our models; there are thus no models, and so no countermodels, and so every argument is valid.

That's bad, so it seems we ought not allow O into our language. But O also seems to make perfectly good sense. Moreover, we can define O using the very same tools that the paracompletist or glut theorist uses in giving their own model theory, so it does not seem open to them to dismiss O as nonsensical. This is one instance of a *revenge* phenomenon: in giving their theory of paradoxes involving the predicate T, the paracompletist or glut theorist invokes machinery (their model theory) that can itself be developed into new paradoxes, paradoxes that the machinery cannot itself dispel.

The threat of new paradoxes illustrates another facet of this sort of objection. One motivation for developing either paraconsistent or paracomplete theories was to provide truth predicates that apply to the entirety of the language they are in, without restriction. We might want this because we think our languages can state many (all?) of their own semantic properties, using native expressions like "is true." Though K3TT and LPTT achieve this in certain respect, they do so at a cost. The cost is introducing other semantic facts, like the ones stated by O, which they cannot express. Have we then gotten all the expressive power we are after, or merely shifted the problem from one about T to one about O?

Responses to this worry tend to start from the observation that model theory, as is it is typically conducted (and as we have conducted it in this chapter), is done within classical logic, using the tools of classical set theory, while the views in question do not take classical logic to be unrestrictedly valid. In particular, paracompletists and glut theorists avoid using full classical reasoning around paradoxes of various sorts. One way of developing this strategy, advocated by Beall (2009); Field (2008), has it that classical reasoning around models, even for languages involving vocabulary like O, is perfectly legitimate, but can only tell us about our own language indirectly, and this indirectness allows O to be no problem. Another way, advocated by Priest (2006b), has it that reasoning about models can tell us much more directly about our language, but that this reasoning about models must itself be done according to nonclassical scruples.[21] It is contentious whether these responses work; for more discussion, see Beall (2008b).

---

[21] Note that the previous reasoning about ζ needed to assume both 1) that either ζ takes value 1 or it takes some other value and 2) that if it takes more than one value, something has gone wrong. These are not far from LEM and explosion, respectively.

CHAPTER SIX

Classical Logic
Restricted Capture–Release

We have now seen a range of options for responding to the Liar paradox by offering alternatives to classical logic. There are also a number of approaches that work within classical logic, trying to find other ways to defuse the paradox. We review some of those options in this chapter. In keeping with the strategy of this book, we will provide some representative ideas, rather than a full survey.

6.1 Classical logic

One hallmark of the approaches we will discuss in this chapter is a willingness to somehow *restrict* the range of application of capture and release, to block the paradoxical reasoning. This is antithetical to some approaches to truth, especially those that take unrestricted capture and release to be its defining characteristics. But it is consonant with other approaches, like some of those that take the main feature of truth to be that it reports a non-trivial semantic property of sentences (e.g., corresponding with a fact in the world, or having a value in a model).

As we saw in our analysis of the Liar reasoning, given the understanding of "classical" we have adopted, in the presence of classical logic there is no choice but to restrict capture or release in some ways. The status of classical logic is, of course, a substantial philosophical issue in itself, but we note three reasons one might wish to keep it. First, and most contentious, one might hold a philosophical position according to which classical logic is simply correct, and other logics are not. But second, and much less contentious, one might observe the great utility of classical logic, in such settings as the foundations of mathematics, and wish to integrate the theory of truth into that setting. Third, there are other pragmatic motivations, such as the difficulties of developing meta-theory or arithmetic in non-classical settings. Classical logic has been more widely and thoroughly studied than any other logical system we discuss in this book; it's nice to be able to stand on the shoulders at the top of such a large human pyramid![1]

If we adopt a classical logic, we will have to somehow weaken capture or release. It turns out there are a great many ways this can be done. We will review some of the leading approaches here. In this chapter, classical logic is always assumed, and $\models$ is taken to be the classical (first order) consequence relation.

6.2 Tarski's hierarchy of languages

6.2.1 Basic motivation

Traditionally, the main avenue for resolving the paradox within classical logic is Tarski's hierarchy of languages and meta-languages. Tarski (1935, 1944) concluded from the paradox that no language could contain its own truth predicate (in his terminology, no language can be "semantically closed"). The reasoning of §3.1.3.3 illustrates this, as it supposes a truth predicate which applies to

---

[1] We are sure this is the metaphor Newton would have preferred, if he had only gone to summer camp.

sentences of the language it is in, including the Liar sentence, and reasons from there to a contradiction.

Of course, if a language does *not* contain its own truth predicate, then problematic sentences like the Liar sentence cannot be constructed, and the paradox is resolved. This is the core of the Tarskian approach.

6.2.2 A formal picture

To implement this idea, Tarski proposed that we start with a language that contains *no* truth predicate. For reasons that will become clear in a moment, call this language $\mathcal{L}_0$. $\mathcal{L}_0$ is an interpreted language: say the language of arithmetic.[2] $\mathcal{L}_0$ is interpreted by a classical model, which assigns an extension to each predicate and function, and a value to each term. We will write classical models as $\mathfrak{M}$. We let $\mathcal{L}_0$ be interpreted by the standard model of arithmetic, which we call $\mathbb{N}$.

Some sentences of $\mathcal{L}_0$ are true in this model, and others are not; they are false in this model. (No sentence is both.) Of course, truth in a model is not *truth*. But classical theorists often take truth in a model to tell us something about truth *itself*, something we can exploit as we provide theories of truth. This is all the more the case when the model in question is something like $\mathbb{N}$, a model we trust to get a great deal *right*; for sentences of $\mathcal{L}_0$, there is only a slim difference if any between being true in $\mathbb{N}$ and just being *true*. We will treat them as the same.

---

[2] In general, we may assume the syntax of $\mathcal{L}_0$ is that of arithmetic, or that it contains any of the other devices for referring to sentences discussed in Chapter 4; in fact, the particular mechanism Tarski himself outlined is another one entirely, which we will not discuss here. Here we'll just use the language of arithmetic.

$\mathcal{L}_0$ has no truth predicate. But, since it is interpreted in $\mathbb{N}$, there are facts about which of its sentences are true or false. So, we can certainly talk about truth for $\mathcal{L}_0$ (as we have been doing); we just can't do so in $\mathcal{L}_0$ itself. To formalize this talk, we can "step up" to an expanded language $\mathcal{L}_1$, which contains a truth predicate, but one that only applies to sentences of $\mathcal{L}_0$. That is, $\mathcal{L}_1$ is the language of arithmetic augmented with an extra atomic predicate T_0.[3]

With this restriction, it is easy enough to define a truth predicate which completely accurately states the truth values of every sentence in $\mathcal{L}_0$ (again, as interpreted in $\mathbb{N}$). This will obey release and a restricted version of capture, and it yields no paradox.

In fact, it's possible to implicitly define truth for $\mathcal{L}_0$ in $\mathcal{L}_1$. Recall that the language of arithmetic contains a term $\underline{o}$, and functions $S, +,$ and $\times$, but no predicates other than $=$. Hence, all atomic sentences of $\mathcal{L}_0$ are identities between possibly complex terms. To define truth for atomic sentences like this, we only need to define a denotation function for terms, which we will write with a postfix $^\circ$. This can be done in $\mathcal{L}_0$, but because it is not all that informative about truth, we will skip the details.[4] What is important is that when a (closed) term t of $\mathcal{L}_0$ denotes a number n, we can prove $t^\circ = \underline{n}$, and that when it does not, we can prove $t^\circ \neq \underline{n}$.[5]

Using this function, we can define truth for atomic sentences, by in effect stating the T-schema (combining capture and release with the material conditional) for atomic sentences. Recall that in the

---

[3] All the terms we have available are still only terms for numbers, so when we say that T_0 "only applies" to sentences of $\mathcal{L}_0$, we mean that $T_0(t)$ is only ever *true* when t denotes the code number of a sentence of $\mathcal{L}_0$. Tarksi himself took a different approach, on which reference to languages was achieved *directly*, not via code numbers; on Tarski's approach, $\mathcal{L}_1$ simply contains no term at all for any sentence containing T_0, so there can be no attempt to predicate T_0 of such a term in $\mathcal{L}_1$.

[4] See Halbach (2011); McGee (1991) for careful presentations.

[5] Recall from Chapter 4 that $\underline{n}$ is the term with n many copies of S applied to $\underline{o}$.

language of arithmetic, the only predicate is identity, so what we need is:

1. $\forall s \forall t (T(s \dot{=} t) \equiv s^\circ = t^\circ)$

We build up from there using the compositional principles we introduced in Chapter 4:

2. $\forall x (\text{sent}(x) \supset (T(\dot{\neg} x) \equiv \neg T(x)))$
3. $\forall x \forall y (\text{sent}(x \dot{\wedge} y) \supset (T(x \dot{\wedge} y) \equiv T(x) \wedge T(y)))$
4. $\forall v \forall x (\text{sent}(\dot{\forall} v x) \supset (T(\dot{\forall} v x) \equiv \forall t T(x(v/t))))$

As these combine the compositional truth principles with a clause for atomic sentences of arithmetic, call them the CT-rules.

These rules can used in several ways, but the main idea is that they implicitly define truth for $\mathcal{L}_0$. Tarski showed that this implicit definition can be made explicit, by a familiar trick. The set of true sentences of $\mathcal{L}_0$ is the smallest set that obeys the CT-rules. This idea can be implemented in second-order arithmetic, or in set theory. Replace each occurrence of T in CT-rules with a second order variable X. Call this $CT(X)$. Then we can define $T_0(y)$ as $\forall X (CT(X) \supset X(y))$. This is the second-order definition of truth provided by Tarski.

This defines a set of sentences $T_0 \subseteq \mathcal{L}_0$.[6] We can use that set to interpret $\mathcal{L}_1$, which has a truth predicate for sentences of $\mathcal{L}_0$. For a given model $\mathfrak{M}$ for $\mathcal{L}_0$, we can expand it to a model $\langle \mathfrak{M}, T_0 \rangle$ for the language $\mathcal{L}_1$. As usual, the intended model is $\langle \mathbb{N}, T_0 \rangle$.

---

[6] That is, it defines such a set given a coding scheme for $\mathcal{L}_0$ and a model of $\mathcal{L}_0$. As is traditional, we suppress most explicit mention of this relativity. We suppress relativity to the coding scheme because it mostly doesn't matter (at least among reasonable choices of scheme), and relativity to the model because we really mainly have $\mathbb{N}$ in mind.

There is no need to stop there. If we want to describe truth in $\mathcal{L}_1$, we can step up to $\mathcal{L}_2$ to get a truth predicate for $\mathcal{L}_1$. And so on. Most hierarchy theorists see this process as going on indefinitely. The hierarchy never ends! At each stage, a new (interpreted) language is produced, which expresses truth for the languages below it in the hierarchy. Mathematically, it can be quite complicated to try to model this. We will at least need to run the hierarchy through all the natural numbers. If you know some set theory, you will see that if we want to model open-endedness, we cannot stop there, and will need to push through transfinite ordinals. Doing that produces some mathematical complications, and raises philosophical ones about what counts as really modeling open-endedness.[7]

Why is there no Liar paradox in this sort of hierarchy of languages? Because while the predicate T_{n-1} introduced at any level n obeys capture and release for sentences of $\mathcal{L}_{n-1}$, it does not obey capture for all sentences of $\mathcal{L}_n$. $T_{n-1}\langle A \rangle$ is always false, when A is a sentence of $\mathcal{L}_n$ but not of $\mathcal{L}_{n-1}$. So, if A is true, we have a counterexample to capture. In such a case, it will turn out that $T_n \langle A \rangle$ is true—but this is not a sentence of $\mathcal{L}_n$ at all, only of $\mathcal{L}_{n+1}$ and above.

It will help to think through what a "Liar sentence" in such a hierarchy might be. It should be a sentence λ such that $\lambda \equiv \neg T \langle \lambda \rangle$; but which truth predicate is this? Let n be the least number such that $\lambda \in \mathcal{L}_n$; then the truth predicate in question must be T_m for some $m < n$, since no other truth predicates are yet available. Such a "Liar sentence" is simply true. It is the negation of $T_m \langle \lambda \rangle$, and this is the application of a restricted truth predicate to something *outside*

---

[7] See Halbach (1997); McGee (1991) for discussion of the mathematical issues. For less technical development of this approach, and critical discussion, see Soames (1999).

its extension. This application is false, and so its negation, which is equivalent to λ, is true. No paradox arises.[8]

6.2.3 Common objections

Tarski's hierarchical approach has been subject to a number of criticisms. One is that in light of naturally occurring cases of self-reference, insisting that all self-applications of truth be false (or somehow not well-formed) seems overly drastic. Though Tarski himself was more concerned to resolve the Liar for formal languages, his solution seems implausible as applied to many naturally occurring uses of "true."

Another important problem was highlighted in Kripke (1975). As Kripke notes, any syntactically fixed set of levels will make it extremely hard, if not impossible, to place various non-paradoxical claims within the hierarchy in anything approaching a plausible way. For instance, if Jc says that *everything Michael says is true*, the claim has to be made from a level of the hierarchy (call it j) higher than everything Michael says. And, if among the things Michael says is that *everything Dave says is true*, then this claim must be at a higher level (call it m) than all of Dave's claims. Thus, Jc's original claim too is at a higher level than all of Dave's claims. But now, if among the things Dave says is that *everything Jc says is true*, then this claim must be at a higher level (call it d) than all of Jc's claims. We have a circle: $j > m > d > j$. This is impossible. But without such a

---

[8] In Tarski's original presentation, and many that follow it, the Liar sentence is not syntactically well-formed. Intuitively, a truth predicate T_{n-1} is only supposed to apply to sentences of $\mathcal{L}_{n-1}$, and so it is not supposed to be coherent to apply it to sentences in $\mathcal{L}_n$ that are not in $\mathcal{L}_{n-1}$. Such syntactic restrictions can be imposed in various ways, and are part of the motivation for the Tarskian hierarchy. But the use of numerical coding makes them slightly awkward. The fact that our attempt to form "Liar sentences" winds up with something non-problematically true is a reflection of those syntactic constraints.

circle, at least one of these claims won't work as intended, on the Tarskian theory; it will be false, *even if* all the claims it calls true really are true.

In light of these sorts of problems, many have concluded that Tarski's hierarchy of languages and meta-languages buys a solution to the Liar paradox at the cost of implausible restrictiveness, at least if it is seen as providing a theory of the truth predicates we ordinarily and freely use.[9]

6.3 Proof theory for self-applicative truth

6.3.1 Basic motivation

Tarski's hierarchy is drastically restrictive, preventing any application of a truth predicate to a sentence containing that truth predicate from working as it should. We have seen that this appears unpalatable, and we would like to find more realistic alternatives.

Since we are still assuming classical logic, we must find some other way to weaken capture and release. But it would be nice to find a way that avoids the extreme restrictions Tarski proposed. We thus need to find a way to have a classical language with a truth predicate that applies sensibly to its own sentences as much as is possible. Likewise, we would like to avoid a hierarchy of languages, as much as is possible.

There are a number of techniques which can be used to do this. First, we will consider a proof-theoretic approach, which tries to develop axiomatic theories for a language containing its own truth predicate, supposing classical logic. Recall, the Tarskian approach to defining truth started with a set of principles about

---

[9] See also the discussions of Field (2008); Horsten (2011); Priest (2006b); Scharp (2013).

truth for atomic sentences and how truth composes, which we called the CT-rules. But those rules could just as well be taken to be axioms of a theory. And indeed, that theory has been explored in depth, construed as a set of axioms added to the base theory PA.[10]

Our goal now is to do something similar for a language which contains its own truth predicate. Of course, we do not expect to get everything we might want. By and large, the idea is to keep some form of the compositional principles, or some limited forms of capture and release themselves.

6.3.2 A formal picture

To develop such a theory, let us continue to keep the background logic fully classical. We will also continue to treat $\mathcal{L}$ as the language of arithmetic, and start with Peano arithmetic PA as our base theory. We add a truth predicate T to $\mathcal{L}$, forming $\mathcal{L}^+$. Unlike the Tarskian case, there is only a single truth predicate here, and it will apply to every formula in $\mathcal{L}^+$ in the same way; we do not have anything like a hierarchy here.[11]

How can we build a workable theory of truth over PA in $\mathcal{L}^+$? One approach is to try to have as much of CT in $\mathcal{L}^+$ as we can. As it happens, we can have it all: owing to CT's recursive structure, it only

---

[10] There is a subtlety involved in doing so. We need to decide how to treat induction in the new theory. This turns out to be an important issue, and the strength of the resulting theory depends a great deal on the choice. If we include formulas with T in the induction schema, we get a reasonably strong theory, sometimes known as CT, while if we do not, we get a conservative extension of PA. For more discussion of this, see Feferman (1991); Halbach (2011); Horsten (2011).

[11] As we mentioned in footnote 10, we need to decide how to extend PA to $\mathcal{L}^+$. Though we will not go into enough detail for it to matter, for the record, we will extend the induction schema to all of $\mathcal{L}^+$, including those formulas containing T.

tells us about the results of applying T to (codes for) formulas that do not themselves contain T. The result is safe from paradox, but for entirely uninteresting reasons: T is not constrained at all in its applications to (codes for) formulas that contain it.

The problem is that now that we are working with $\mathcal{L}^+$, this is too much of a restriction. The result is very weak as a theory of truth; it tells us virtually nothing about iterated applications of the truth predicate. It does not prove $T\langle T\langle o = o \rangle \rangle$, for instance. This is just the sort of thing we wanted to get out of our theory for $\mathcal{L}^+$, so what we have is clearly not good enough.

One way to strengthen our theory is to add two rules:

$$\frac{A}{T\langle A \rangle} \qquad \frac{T\langle A \rangle}{A}$$

The first rule is called "necessitation," and the second "co-necessitation." These look like capture and release, respectively, but they are importantly different. Their names should remind you of similar rules from modal logic; and like these similar rules, these must be understood with some care.

The deduction theorem holds for the kind of classical logic we are using: if $A \vdash B$, then $\vdash A \rightarrow B$. Thus, if these rules were allowed to be used in proofs from premises, we would simply get the T-schema back, and we would have inconsistency. The way to understand these rules, then, is as *closure conditions on theories*. If a theory already proves A, the rules tell us, then it also proves $T\langle A \rangle$, and the same for $T\langle A \rangle$ and A. You have to have a proof already in hand to apply the rules. These rules thus have the same status as usual formulations of the rules of universal generalization or uniform substitution. (In Smiley's terminology, they are *rules of proof* rather than *rules of inference*.)

If we take the rules of CT formulated in $\mathcal{L}^+$ (so that the compositional rules are stated in terms of $\text{sent}_{\mathcal{L}^+}$ rather than sent), added to our $\mathcal{L}^+$ version of *PA*, and close under necessitation and co-necessitation, we get a fairly nice theory of truth. It is known as *FS*, for Friedman and Sheard (1987), who first described it.[12]

FS has some nice properties. It preserves a great deal of the useful Tarskian truth theory while applying it to $\mathcal{L}^+$. Also, it offers a response to the Liar that some have found plausible: *FS* is mostly silent about the Liar sentence. For example, it proves neither that the Liar is true nor that it is untrue. It thus captures one aspect of the paracomplete idea considered in Chapter 5. Unlike paracomplete approaches, though, *FS* is built in classical logic, and so it *does* provide a proof that the Liar sentence is either true or not; it just doesn't tell us which.

6.3.2.1 COMMON OBJECTIONS

Though *FS* has some nice properties, it also has some significant problems. Perhaps the most widely noted is that though *FS* is consistent, it is *ω-inconsistent*; this means that there is an open sentence $A(x)$ such that FS proves $A(\underline{n})$ for every numeral $\underline{n}$, and also proves $\neg \forall x A(x)$. Because of this, FS has no models where $\mathcal{L}$ is interpreted in $\mathbb{N}$, i.e., where the variables over numbers really range over numbers as intended. Many have found this makes the theory unsatisfactory. The objection is one that needs to be handled with care though. As Halbach shows, though *FS* is ω-inconsistent, it is actually arithmetically sound. Its problems with standard models all stem from the way it handles truth predicates, not facts about the numbers themselves.[13]

---

[12] Friedman and Sheard used a different axiomatization. The current one is due to Halbach (1994), which is a good source for those interested in further discussion of this theory.

[13] See Barrio (2006); Halbach (2011); Horsten (2011); Leitgeb (2007) for further discussion.

6.3.3 *Another formal picture*

FS is not the only way to build a proof theory for truth in $\mathcal{L}^+$. Another way takes a different approach to capturing some aspects of paracompleteness in the classical setting. FS does so by being mostly silent on problematic sentences. We might try instead to build aspects of paracompleteness into our theory more directly.

How can we do that proof-theoretically, using classical logic? Intuitively, we want to treat truth and falsehood separately, just as having the value $\frac{1}{2}$ in logics like K3 and LP makes the value 0 different from not having the value 1. So, we might want to introduce a new predicate F for falsehood. If we do that, it is important to make sure our axioms do not tell us that $T\langle A\rangle \equiv \neg F\langle A\rangle$. That would defeat the purpose of capturing some aspects of paracompleteness. It turns out we do not need to do this, however. We can *define* $F\langle A\rangle$ to be $T\langle \neg A\rangle$. But if we are to do this, and make sure we don't get $T\langle A\rangle \equiv \neg F\langle A\rangle$, we have to be very careful about how our axioms describe the way truth interacts with negation. That is just what our theory does. It does so by axioms which treat negated and unnegated sentences separately. One widely used set of axioms is as follows:

1. $\forall s \forall t (T(s \doteq t) \equiv s^{\circ} = t^{\circ})$
2. $\forall s \forall t (T(\neg s \doteq t) \equiv s^{\circ} \neq t^{\circ})$
3. $\forall x (\operatorname{sent}_{\mathcal{L}^+}(x) \supset (T(\neg \neg x) \equiv T(x)))$
4. $\forall x \forall y (\operatorname{sent}_{\mathcal{L}^+}(x \wedge y) \supset (T(x \wedge y) \equiv T(x) \wedge T(y)))$
5. $\forall x \forall y (\operatorname{sent}_{\mathcal{L}^+}(x \wedge y) \supset (T(\neg(x \wedge y)) \equiv (T(\neg x) \vee T(\neg y))))$
6. $\forall v \forall x (\operatorname{sent}_{\mathcal{L}^+}(\forall vx) \supset (T(\forall vx) \equiv \forall t T(x(t/v))))$
7. $\forall v \forall x (\operatorname{sent}_{\mathcal{L}^+}(\forall vx) \supset (T(\neg \forall vx) \equiv \exists t T(\neg x(t/v))))$
8. $\forall t (T(T(t)) \equiv T(t^{\circ}))$
9. $\forall t (T(\neg T(t)) \equiv (T(\neg t^{\circ}) \vee \neg \operatorname{sent}_{\mathcal{L}^+}(t^{\circ})))$

Some versions of the theory also add $\forall x(\mathrm{sent}_{\mathcal{L}^+}(x) \supset \neg(T(x) \wedge T(\dot{\neg}x)))$.[14]

If we add these axioms to our theory PA in $\mathcal{L}^+$, with induction extended to all formulas of $\mathcal{L}^+$, we get the theory known as KF, for Kripke–Feferman.[15]

KF has some nice properties. Perhaps most importantly, it is an axiomatization of the Kripke fixed-point idea we used to construct Kleene–Kripke models. More specifically, models of KF are exactly the ones you build out of the fixed point construction we sketched in Chapter 5. As we noted there, there are many such models, and they are all models of KF. KF is a reasonably strong theory, which is known to be equivalent in strength to a modest fragment of second-order arithmetic. KF also illustrates how ideas of partiality, related to paracomplete theories, can also be implemented in a classical setting.

Before turning to objections, we pause to mention one way proof-theoretic approaches are both flexible and delicate. We mentioned in Chapter 4 that we prefer theories which can generalize from truth to satisfaction, or "true of." Proof theory can provide such a generalization, since we can include *parameters* in formulas to which T applies. We note, though, that the proof-theoretic properties of the resulting theories can be a complicated matter, and it is not safe to assume they are just the same as the ones without parameters.

---

[14] Our formulation of KF again follows Halbach (2011), from whom we also borrow the notation t°. Note that, for these axioms, the connectives $\supset$ and $\vee$ should be understood as defined from $\neg$ and $\wedge$ in the usual ways; that way, it is not a problem that we have not included axioms for handling applications of T to sentences involving them.

[15] This theory is described in Feferman (1991), which draws on unpublished work which was circulated earlier. It was also in effect outlined in McGee (1991) and Reinhardt (1986). Again, Halbach (2011) is a good starting place for readers interested in further discussion of this theory.

Though *KF* is a very elegant theory, it is not without its drawbacks. Though it is fairly strong, it is not so strong as to allow us to develop a great deal of classical mathematics, for one thing.

This sort of concern may not matter all that much, as our starting point was merely *PA*, and perhaps asking our theory of truth to generate a great deal of mathematics may be unreasonable. (It's meant to be a theory of *truth*, after all, not mathematics!) But on the properties of truth itself, *KF* also has some features some have found undesirable.

One example (discussed at length in Horsten 2011) is that $KF \vdash \lambda \wedge \neg T \langle \lambda \rangle$. Unlike *FS*, *KF* gives us a verdict on Liars. But it seems to then deny its own accuracy, as it first proves λ, and then denies its truth. This makes the truth predicate of *KF* awkward in some important ways.[16]

6.4 Model theory for classical truth

Classical-logic-based approaches to truth need not proceed axiomatically, like the previous approaches have. In this section, we consider some model-theoretic ways to provide classical logic with a truth predicate.

6.4.1 A formal picture

Our discussion of *KF* already indicates how we might proceed. Though in defining Kleene–Kripke models, we used a 3-valued valuation scheme, which led to non-classical logics K3 and LP, there

---

[16] See also Field (2008); Maudlin (2004); Reinhardt (1986), for further discussion.

is nothing else fundamentally non-classical about the Kripkean apparatus. Indeed, the way we formulated *KF* more or less tells us how we can re-do the Kripke construction in a classical setting.

Recall from Chapter 5 that a Kleene–Kripke model $\langle D, I' \rangle$ interprets T as a Kleene–Kripke fixed point. This guarantees that $I'(T\langle A \rangle) = I'(A)$. I' assigns values from $\{0, \frac{1}{2}, 1\}$, where on one interpretation, 1 stands for true, 0 for false, and $\frac{1}{2}$ is some sort of gap. We noted in Chapter 5 that the paracomplete nature of K3 comes not simply from the value $\frac{1}{2}$, but the structure of the resulting logic. For classical purposes, we will focus on a way of capturing some of the effects of $\frac{1}{2}$, without departing from classical logic. The way to do so is to think of the predicate T as *partial*, in that it applies to some sentences, does not apply to some, and is simply silent on others. (This is, of course, still a non-classical idea, but it is a useful halfway point.) This idea can be extracted from the structure of Kleene–Kripke models. Let $\mathcal{E} = \{A : I'(T\langle A \rangle) = 1\} = \{A : I'(A) = 1\}$. Let $\mathcal{A} = \{A : I'(T\langle A \rangle) = 0\} = \{A : I'(A) = 0\}$. $\mathcal{E}$ is the set of things T is true of, and is called the *extension* of T. $\mathcal{A}$ is the set of things T is not true of, and is called the *anti-extension* of T. Sentences like the Liar sentence are in neither $\mathcal{E}$ nor $\mathcal{A}$. In Kleene–Kripke models, these were assigned the value $\frac{1}{2}$. That is how we worked out our models in a nonclassical setting, but $\mathcal{E}$ and $\mathcal{A}$ are just two sets, and there is nothing that stop us from using them in classical settings as well.

So, let us try now to return to a fully classical setting, where $\mathcal{L}^+$ is the language of arithmetic, extended by T. Our model $\langle D, I' \rangle$ is the standard model of arithmetic $\mathbb{N}$, extended by the Kleene–Kripke minimal fixed point. In this setting, recall, our sentence names and numbers may be the same, if we use Gödel coding. For this reason, we need to work with codes rather than sentences, and it is convenient to throw the numbers that are not sentence codes into $\mathcal{A}$. So, we can redefine:

$$\mathcal{E} = \{\langle A \rangle : I'(A) = 1\}$$
$$\mathcal{A} = \{\langle A \rangle : I'(A) = 0\} \cup \{\underline{n} : \neg\mathsf{sent}_{\mathcal{L}^+}(n)\}$$

$\langle \mathbb{N}, \langle \mathcal{E}, \mathcal{A} \rangle \rangle$ is a *partial model* for $\mathcal{L}^+$.

We are not quite there yet, since a partial model like this is not fully classical. It treats all T-free sentences classically, as well as a good number of T-involving sentences, but there will be sentences (like λ) that still do not take a classical value; as such, we will need to invoke some non-classical valuation scheme to determine the truth of complex sentences in it.

But, following an idea in Parsons (1974), we can just forget about $\mathcal{A}$ entirely, and use $\mathcal{E}$ on its own to create a classical model. $\langle \mathbb{N}, \mathcal{E} \rangle$ is a fully classical model of $\mathcal{L}^+$. This is called the "closed-off" Kripke construction, as the gap between extension and anti-extension is closed off by throwing everything in the gap into the false category of a classical model.

We know this model cannot make true all of capture and release. But it does make a restricted form true. The following holds in the closed-off model:

$$[T\langle A \rangle \vee T\langle \neg A \rangle] \supset [T\langle A \rangle \equiv A]$$

This tells us that capture and release (in the form of the T-schema) holds for sentences that are well-behaved, in the sense of satisfying $T\langle A \rangle \vee T\langle \neg A \rangle$.

What happens to the Liar sentence with this approach? As in the three-valued case, the Liar is interpreted as falling within the gap. λ is neither in $\mathcal{E}$ nor $\mathcal{A}$. The sentence λ thus falls outside of the domain where T is interpreted as well-behaved. Because the situation is classical, and $\langle\lambda\rangle \notin \mathcal{E}$, we know that $\neg T\langle\lambda\rangle$ is true in the closed-off model; likewise, so is $\neg T\langle\neg\lambda\rangle$; the Liar sentence is not true, and neither is its negation.

On well-behaved sentences, we have the fixed-point property that A and $T\langle A\rangle$ have the same truth value, and so the semantics of $\mathcal{L}^+$ and the semantics it assigns to T correspond exactly. On pathological sentences like λ, they do not, and indeed, cannot, at pain of triviality.

We've detoured through a paracomplete construction to build $\mathcal{E}$. But, as was observed in Feferman (1984), we can build this extension without explicitly invoking non-classical valuation schemes at all. The trick is to mimic the way we defined a Tarskian truth predicate via the CT-rules in §6.2.2, but instead of the CT-rules, use a set of rules very close to KF, which as we know from §6.3.3, mimics partiality by careful treatment of negation. We'll skip the details; see Feferman (1984); McGee (1991).

6.4.2 Common objections

The closed-off Kripke construction is vulnerable to similar objections to the ones raised for KF, since they are, after all, based on the same ideas. We have already noted that the model makes $\neg T\langle\lambda\rangle$ (and $\neg T\langle\neg\lambda\rangle$) true. This illustrates that, on certain pathological sentences, closed-off Kripke models are not very well behaved. Recall that $\neg T\langle\lambda\rangle$ entails λ, so λ itself is true on all of these models—yet so is the claim that it is not!

Defenders of the approach argue that this simply reflects the non-well-behaved status of the sentences involved, but it does show that, as an analysis of truth for $\mathcal{L}^+$, the closed-off construction is only partially successful; as with KF, we can see that our model validates $\lambda \wedge \neg T\langle\lambda\rangle$, by the definition of λ via the fixed-point lemma. Hence, like *KF*, the model-theoretic closed-off Kripke construction cannot accurately report its own results, and indeed goes so far as to deny some of them. Thus, as an attempt at a complete theory of truth, the closed-off construction can be argued to fall short. For further discussion, see Field (2008); Glanzberg (2015); Maudlin (2004).

6.5 Contextualist approaches

Another family of proposed solutions to the Liar are *contextualist solutions*. These also make use of classical logic, but base their solutions primarily on some ideas from the philosophy of language. They take the basic lesson of the Liar to be that Liar sentences show some form of *context dependence*, even in otherwise non-context-dependent fragments of a language. They seek to explain how this can be so, and rely on it to resolve the problems raised by the Liar.

Contextualist theories share with a number of approaches we have already seen the idea that there is something indeterminate or semantically fishy about our Liar sentence λ. But contextualist views often give a special role to issues of "revenge."

6.5.1 Basic motivation

Let us start with the paracomplete idea that sentences like the Liar sentence are gappy. As we discussed in Chapter 5, it is not entirely straightforward to spell out what this status is, but it might be explained as one that *denies* truth and falsity to sentences like the Liar. Contextualists, assuming a classical perspective (more or less), try to express this by saying that these sentences fail to have truth values, or fail to have well-behaved truth values. But in a classical setting, we do not want to say they have some non-classical value, or invoke a special notion of denial;[17] rather, we want to say they really fail to have any kind of truth value at all.

One classical way to understand this kind of non-well-behaved status is to suppose that Liar sentences lack truth values in a straightforward way. They lack truth values because they fail to provide well-defined truth bearers to have truth values. They thus lack truth values in much the same way sticks and stones do. To make this vivid (as discussed in Glanzberg (2001); Parsons (1974)), suppose that truth bearers are propositions expressed by sentences in contexts, and that the Liar sentence fails to express a proposition. Though this is probably not what the paracomplete approach had in mind, it is a natural gloss on failing to be true and failing to be false. It is thus the beginning of a classical account of how the Liar winds up lacking a well-behaved truth value.

As we have seen in several ways in this chapter, classical approaches to truth restrict capture and release in some way or another. Continuing along the lines we have just begun, we could say that capture and release fail to apply to the Liar precisely because there is no truth bearer, and so nothing for truth to work on (capture and release do not apply to sticks or stones either, unless you are a collector!).[18]

So far, what we have described is a classical gloss on the para-complete idea of gaps. But, as the contextualists see it, this is an *unstable* proposal. After all, if the Liar sentence doesn't express a proposition at all, then it doesn't express a true proposition. But this is, according to the approach we are now considering, essentially what the Liar sentence says, so it is true after all. We reason from

---

[17] The kind of denial supposed by some paracomplete approaches is difficult to formalize in a classical setting.

[18] For a somewhat different version of this idea, see van Fraassen (1966, 1968).

failing to have a well-defined truth value to being true. But if the Liar sentence is true, then it has a well-defined truth value, and so capture and release should apply, and we are back in paradox.

Let us review this reasoning a little more carefully. Consider the following sentence:

(ELiar)   ELiar does not express a true proposition.

In a setting where we talk about expressing propositions, this is the correct form of the Liar sentence. We reason as follows. If ELiar expresses a proposition at all, that proposition is true if and only if it is not true, by the by-now-familiar reasoning in §3.1.3.3.[19] So, by logic, we conclude that ELiar doesn't express a proposition. Notice, this is not a hypothesis; we have proved that ELiar does not express a proposition. But then by logic again, we can prove that ELiar doesn't express a true proposition. Since this is exactly what ELiar says, we have proved ELiar. There appears to be nothing wrong with our proof, and so, we should take it as proved that ELiar is true. It then does express a proposition, as that is the only way it can be true. So, we are right back in paradox.[20]

A number of non-classical approaches, especially paracomplete ones as we discussed in Chapter 5, see the issue here as an additional revenge problem, along the lines of §5.4.2 and §5.4.3. In contrast, contextualists see it as the basic problem posed by the Liar. The mere fact that a sentence like ELiar does not express a proposition is not especially puzzling. Though we might want to undertand why not, lots of things don't and that does not launch us on long

---

[19] We need to modify capture and release to work with propositions, but the modification is straightforward.

[20] For formal versions of this reasoning, see Glanzberg (2001, 2004a).

logical quests. The problem is that the status of failing to express a proposition is not stable, and anything we do about it seems to land us back in paradox.

It is natural to put this issue in terms of expressing propositions, as that gives a natural classical analysis of gap status or a lack of well-defined truth value. But the basic problem here is more general. The reasoning on display here involves two key steps. First, assigning the Liar semantically defective status: being gappy, failing to express a proposition, being somehow indeterminate, or being semantically defective in some way. Second, concluding from the first step that the Liar must be true, and so not defective or gappy after all. Assuming capture and release apply to non-defective sentences, this results in paradox. So long as we suppose, as the classical perspective often does, that defective status licences the inference that a sentence is not true, then we can reason from the first step to the second. From such a classical perspective, both steps are the result of sound reasoning, and so the conclusions of both steps must be true.

The basic issue here is instability: the Liar sentence is unstable, in that if we assign it defective status, we are forced to assign it truth, and so non-defective status. The main problem of the Liar, according to a contextualist, is to explain how this can be, and in particular how the second step can be non-paradoxical. (Such reasoning is explored in Glanzberg (2001, 2004c); Parsons (1974). For a critical discussion, see Gauker (2006).)

Thus, contextualists seek to explain how the Liar sentence can have unstable semantic status, switching from defective to non-defective in the course of this sort of inference. They do so by appealing to the role of *context* in fixing the semantic status of sentences. Sentences can have different semantic statuses in different contexts. Thus, to contextualists, there must be some non-trivial effect of context involved in the Liar sentence, and more generally, in predications of truth.

6.5.2 A formal picture

Contextualist approaches to the Liar invoke a lot of ideas from philosophy of language; including, in some cases, ideas about sentences expressing propositions in contexts. As we just saw, this is not the contextualist's most basic insight about truth and paradox—the most basic insight is about the instability of Liar sentences. The apparatus from philosophy of language makes it easier to articulate that insight.

How are we to capture this in a formal theory? The most direct route, given the way we have motivated contextualism, would be to develop a formal theory involving contexts, propositions, and so on. This has been done, most extensively by Barwise and Etchemendy (1987) and by Glanzberg (2004a), following ideas of Parsons (1974). But that involves a whole lot of extra issues, not to mention a whole lot of extra mathematics. For the most part, we'll focus on a simpler way to formally capture the contextualist view, that relies on apparatus we have already developed.

A simple way to present a contextualist theory is to start with the idea that the Tarskian hierarchy itself offers a way to see the truth predicate as context dependent.[21] Recall from Chapter 3 that to build a Liar paradox, we need a truth predicate, some way to refer sentences and achieve self-reference, and often negation. The latter do not suggest anything to do with context dependence that might help us with the Liar paradox. So, we might propose that the truth predicate itself is context dependent. After all, the instability we

[21] The version of contextualism we present here loosely follows Burge (1979). Burge's approach is developed further by Koons (1992); Simmons (1993).

just observed seems to show that what is true changes from context to context.

Let us mark this by putting a subscript on the truth predicate, which will now appear as T_i. We can think of i as a contextual parameter that influences how T is interpreted in any given context. The details of how context dependence is introduced will not be of great importance, so long as we have T winding up context dependent somehow.

This should remind you of the Tarski hierarchy of languages, that also has truth predicates with subscripts. And indeed, we will make use of Tarski's hierarchy to interpret our truth predicate. But as now i is a contextual parameter, there is only one predicate T_i, and so only one language in sight. The interpretation of T_i changes from context to context, just like the interpretation of the word "that" does; but there is only one truth predicate just like there is only one word "that."

How are we to interpret T_i in different contexts? Here, Tarski's hierarchy offers one possible answer. Suppose that the effect of a context on i is to set it to a number n, making T_i interpreted as the Tarskian truth predicate T_n.

Let's try to spell this out a little more. For illustration purposes, we can work within a classical model-theoretic approach. We start with our usual $\mathcal{L}^+$, where $\mathcal{L}$ is the language of arithmetic. $\mathcal{L}^+$ contains a truth predicate T_i. We can begin by interpreting $\mathcal{L}^+$ by the first level of the Tarski hierarchy, i.e., as $\langle \mathbb{N}, T_0 \rangle$.

What happens to the Liar sentence λ in this model? We have already seen several things about it. Most important for the contextualist is that it shows some kind of pathology. In particular, the T-schema fails for λ: the model assigns λ true and $T\langle \lambda \rangle$ false. This, as we have noted, is the mark of pathological sentences.

Here, the contextualist has a particular way of understanding what is happening in the model. Recall, for a contextualist, the i in T_i is a contextual parameter, and there is a pragmatic process that sets the value of i in a context. Our model so far offers us only one option for how to interpret the truth predicate. Our only choice is to interpret it as the first level of the Tarskian hierarchy, which would in effect set the value of i to 0 and make $T_i = T_0$. But setting i this way goes bad on λ, as the T-schema fails, so our attempt to interpret λ in context this way goes bad too. Following Burge, we could impose a pragmatic rule that a sentence must be interpreted in a context in such a way as to have the T-schema come out true for it.[22] This principle fails to be satisfied. So, our attempt to interpret λ in context fails, and λ is ruled pathological.

If that were the whole story, we would be stuck: we have a model that makes the Liar sentence true, but in a pathological way, and a pragmatic principle that says we cannot use it. But, recall, the contextualist thinks this is just a stopover on the way to a better solution. Roughly, as we have seen, we can reason that because it is pathological, and so cannot be true, the Liar sentence is true after all! Of course, it cannot be T_0-true; if it was, we would wind up back in pathology.

If we go up a level in the Tarskian hierarchy, we have the resources to explain this. λ cannot be T_0-true. But if we are careful about how context works, we can make sense of it being

---

[22] Burge calls his version of this principle *verity*, and notes that it is a requirement that a sentence be assigned coherent truth conditions in a context. Burge sees this as a Gricean principle, generating an implicature. There are other ways to capture the problem with the interpretation of λ, as discussed in Barwise and Etchemendy (1987); Gaifman (1992, 2000); Glanzberg (2004c, 2006, 2015). Glanzberg, in particular, notes that we can see a failure of the model to capture the semantic properties of the language, and does not rely on a special pragmatic principle.

T_1-true. It can be true on a wider interpretation of T_i—our context-dependent truth predicate.

To clarify how this works, remember that λ is a context dependent sentence, because it contains a truth predicate. We'll write λ_i to remind us of this.[23] If we try to interpret i as 0 for λ_i, the T-schema for T_0 fails. But let us see what happens with the model for the next level up in the Tarskian hierarchy: $\langle \mathbb{N}, T_0, T_1 \rangle$. In particular, let's look at what this model says about λ_0. We already know the models makes λ_0 true (as we discussed in §6.2.2). As λ_0 is true in $\langle \mathbb{N}, T_0 \rangle$, $\lambda_0 \in T_1$. So, the T_1 version of the T-schema holds for λ_0: the model $\langle \mathbb{N}, T_0, T_1 \rangle$ makes true $T_1 \langle \lambda_0 \rangle \equiv \lambda_0$.

As we discussed previously, the contextualist sees this as a shift in context, which changes the value of i in T_i from 0 to 1. The pragmatics requires us to set the value of i to be 0 in λ_i, but to be 1 for the occurrences of T_i that state the T-schema for λ_i. In the value 1 context, we can correctly say that the Liar sentence as interpreted in the value 0 context is true. As may contextualists have noted, this is in effect to talk about, or reflect on, the way things were working in the prior context.[24] What we can report, from the value 1 context, is the failure of λ to receive a non-pathological interpretation in the value 0 context. But because of what the Liar sentence says, this makes it true, according to the value 1 context. This is just what the reasoning we have already rehearsed requires.

It is important to see how the Tarskian apparatus is being used here. Levels of the Tarskian hierarchy represent contexts, in which

---

[23] The notation here is crude. λ is context dependent because the truth predicate is, so writing the subscript on the sentence marks that there is context dependence somewhere, but does not say where.

[24] See in addition to Burge, Glanzberg (2006, 2015); Parsons (1974), and the critical discussion of Gauker (2006).

the truth predicate is interpreted. As we go up in the hierarchy, we get wider truth predicates, which can assign truth conditions to more sentences. The Tarskian requirement that we have our indices arranged in order, and only non-pathologically apply truth predicates at any given level to the levels below, is now a pragmatic requirement on which assignments of values in contexts allow for coherent interpretations.

On this version of the contextualist approach, we have a genuine hierarchy. It should be clear that it does not stop at level 1. The same reasoning we have just been through can be re-applied to move us to level 2, and then 3, and so on. As we discussed in §6.2, the hierarchy is open-ended—this process never stops![25]

The hierarchy just described is highly stratified, as it keeps all the Tarskian levels. As such, it falls afoul of the objection to hierarchies discussed in §6.2.3. But it is also possible to combine a contextually driven hierarchy with a more coarse-grained stratification that uses more inclusive, self-applicative truth predicates at each level. For instance, we can treat each level of the hierarchy not as Tarskian, but via the closed-off Kripke construction. Rather than interpreting T_i at level 0 as the Tarskian predicate T_0, we can interpret it as $\mathcal{E}$.[26] This gives us levels with much more inclusive predicates, and allows us to account for many examples of the sort we discussed in §6.2.3. Such an approach handles those examples about as well as paracomplete approaches do. Actually, you can take almost any classical option for interpreting a truth predicate you like and use it to interpret the truth predicate at any level. If you prefer proof

[25] Not all contextualists endorse this sort of hierarchy. Notably, Simmons (1993) does not.

[26] Versions of this idea are developed by Burge (1979); Glanzberg (2004a); Parsons (1974). For more discussion of stratification, see Field (2008); Glanzberg (2015).

theory, you can use *FS* or *KF*.[27] Other techniques to minimize pathology can be used as well, such as the networks of pointers in Gaifman (1988, 1992).

6.5.3 *Other Approaches*

We now have an illustration of a contextualist approach. We pause to briefly mention some alternatives, and issues within the contextualist camp.

Most, though as we have mentioned not all, contextualists endorse something like the kind of hierarchy we just discussed, though we have also seen that many contextualists prefer a more coarsely stratified hierarchy than the Tarskian one, and differ on how they should implement it.

The most substantial issues among contextualists relate more to philosophy of language, and so we will mention them only briefly. The main one is how and why the Liar sentence is really context dependent (of course!). Burge, and our Burge-inspired example, places the locus of context dependence in the truth predicate itself. Parsons (1974) and then Glanzberg (2001, 2004*a*) argue it is better to put it in domains of quantification, which are already widely accepted to be context dependent. Quantification enters into predications of truth if we remember that when context dependence is in sight, truth is properly applied to propositions or sentences interpreted in contexts. To say that a sentence *S* is true

---

[27] The main technical challenge here is to be sure you can iterate whatever you use to build a truth predicate. Constructing a hierarchy requires such iteration. This can lead to some pretty complicated mathematics as we move away from Tarskian approaches. Glanzberg (2004*a*) shows how this can be done for the closed-off Kripke construction. Iterating *KF* is discussed in Fujimoto (2011); Jager *et al.* (1999). Some further issues are discussed in Glanzberg (2015).

in context c is to say that *there is* a proposition p expressed by S in c, and the proposition p is true.

Alternatively, Barwise and Etchemendy (1987) and then Groeneveld (1994) argue that the building blocks of propositions, which they call situations, themselves can be used to model the context dependence of the Liar.[28]

6.5.4 Advantages

The main argument in favor of the contextualist approach is that it explains the instability of the Liar sentence we saw previously. As such, it avoids what are commonly seen as revenge problems. Contextualists, as we have already noted, take the instability not to be an additional revenge problem, but the basic issue for the Liar paradox, and build their solutions specifically to solve it.

An added benefit, according to contextualists, is that this can be done while preserving classical logic. As we discussed in Chapter 5, this may not be an unbreakable requirement, but contextualists see it as a benefit.

Finally, contextualists often argue that independently motivated ideas from philosophy of language support the basic contextualist approach.

6.5.5 Common objections

Contextualism faces a number of common objections. Some are, like contextualism itself, driven by philosophy of language. One

[28] Actually, these two approaches have a lot in common. They both need domains of propositions to expand as we move from context to context. For discussion of relations between the situation-theoretic and quantifier-domain approaches, see Glanzberg (2004a). For a detailed match-up between the Barwise and Etchemendy framework and a Burgean framework of indexed truth predicates, see Koons (1992).

asks why we are so sure the Liar sentence is really context dependent, as it does not contain any of the expressions that are normally assumed to be context dependent. Merely noting that such context dependence would avoid paradox does not show that it is present; and especially, does not show that it is present in the natural language instances of the Liar that are the main concern of contextualists. Another asks: if there is context dependence, by what mechanism does it work?[29]

As most contextualist theories endorse some form of hierarchy, they are vulnerable to objections against any hierarchy at all. Contextualists also inherit many challenges related to restrictions on capture and release. Indeed, contextualists will have to provide, for each context, a reasonably good theory of truth. As we have seen, they might invoke any classical approach (or nonclassical, for that matter, although this has been less explored) to explain what that theory is. They will thus inherit many of the weaknesses, as well as the strengths, of those approaches. Contextualists claim these weaknesses are mitigated by the fact that there will be other levels, with stronger theories, but the challenge of finding an adequate classical theory, with or without levels, remain substantial.[30]

Though contextualist solutions are constructed with an eye towards revenge phenomena, it is often argued that they face a revenge problem of their own. If it is possible to quantify over all contexts, then it appears a new revenge problem for contextualists might be constructed (e.g., Juhl, 1997). To retain consistency,

[29] Many of these issues are often mentioned only in passing, but see remarks in Burgess and Burgess (2011); Field (2008); Horsten (2011); Scharp (2013), and the survey by Simmons (2018). Gaifman (1992) asks if the Gricean process Burge uses in his approach does any substantial work in the theory.

[30] See again the discussions in Field (2008); Glanzberg (2015).

contextualists must apply restrictions on quantifiers to such quantifiers as 'all contexts." To achieve this, it must presumably be denied that there are any. Glanzberg (2004b, 2006) argues that this is the correct conclusion, but it is highly controversial. For a survey of thinking about this, see the papers in Rayo and Uzquiano (2006).

6.6 Determinacy revisited

One of the important ideas that informs both paracomplete and classical approaches is that some sentences, like Liar sentences, are somehow indeterminate. We have seen that spelling this idea out can become quite complicated. For paracomplete theorists, as we saw in Chapter 5, the idea is that indeterminacy relates to failures of LEM, and corresponds somehow to the value $\frac{1}{2}$. But we also saw there that the interpretation of this value, and reporting the indeterminate status of sentences like λ, is philosophically delicate. In this chapter, we have seen a number of classical theories that try to capture similar indeterminate status with a background of purely classical logic. With contextualist theories, we saw an attempt to explain indeterminate status instead as some kind of semantic defectiveness, or failure to express a proposition (which is not really an indeterminate status, but a different determinate one). The philosophical explanations of these approaches are equally delicate.

We conclude this chapter by simply noting that this is a central philosophical issue. As this is a book on formal theories, we also note that there have been several attempts to develop formal accounts of determinacy directly. Kripke (1975) offers a way to understand the minimal fixed point as a model of determinacy.[31]

[31] The notion here is called *grounding*, and builds on work of Herzberger (1970).

An extensive theory of (a form of) determinacy in a classical setting is developed by McGee (1991). An extensive theory of (a different form of) determinacy in a paracomplete setting is developed by Field (2008).[32]

---

[32] For critical discussion of McGee, see Glanzberg (2004c). For critical discussion of Field, see Priest (2010); Welch (2008).

CHAPTER SEVEN

Digging Beneath the Structure

This chapter looks at some *substructural* approaches to truth and paradox. These achieve their ends by tinkering with the very shape of consequence itself, in ways we'll explain.

7.1 Deep structure

This section sketches two approaches that use so-called *substructural* logics together with a fully transparent truth predicate. Substructural logics are so-called because they modify the *structural rules* of a logic: rather than modifying the theory of negation, or of the conditional, or of the truth predicate, they instead work at a deeper level, playing with the idea of what it is for an argument to be valid.

One of the approaches we sketch here allows for cases in which consequence fails to be transitive. That is, it allows that there may be formulas *A*, *B*, and *C* such that *A* entails *B* and *B* entails *C*, but such that *A* does not entail *C*. The other allows for cases in which consequence fails to be contractive. That is, it allows that there may be formulas *A* and *B* such that *A* together with *A* entails *B*, but such that a single occurrence of *A* does not entail *B* on its own.

These can seem like surprising properties for a logic to exhibit. But as we will point out, it emerges that allowing for these surprising properties can go a long way towards making a logical environment safe for transparent truth. Moreover, there is a sense in which these approaches allow us to preserve more of classical logic than the non-classical approaches we discussed in Chapter 5. In fact, there is a sense in which the nontransitive approach allows us to preserve all of classical logic.

The approaches are easiest to understand via a particular way of presenting proof systems, which we develop in §7.2 and §7.3. As usual, in §7.4, we go on to consider some of the advantages of these approaches, and in §7.5, we consider some of the objections that defenders of these approaches must face. The two families of approaches have a number of features in common, so we present them alongside each other. Nonetheless, some of the issues we discuss will require distinguishing between the families. When this happens, we will say so.

7.2 A formal framework

Since our goal here is only to give the flavour of these approaches, we give a very rudimentary sketch. In particular, we will only present a fragment of these approaches; the fragment we consider includes only the connectives $\neg$ and $\wedge$. It is entirely possible to extend these approaches to the full usual complement of logical vocabulary, including the usual range of connectives and quantifiers, but we think this little fragment is enough to give the gist.

We present the frameworks using a *sequent calculus*. Our sequent calculi are proof systems that work on *sequents*: objects of the form

$\Gamma : \Delta$, where Γ and Δ are multisets of formulas.[1] In the calculus we present here, we take all sequents of the form $A : A$ as our axioms, and go on to specify a number of rules allowing us to derive new sequents from sequents already derived. In the end, we will count an argument with premises Γ and conclusions Δ as *valid* (and write $\Gamma \vdash \Delta$) iff the sequent $\Gamma : \Delta$ can be derived. Our axioms $A : A$, then ensure directly that the consequence relations we arrive at will be *reflexive*: every formula will validly entail itself.[2]

It may feel slightly unfamiliar to some readers to have sets of sentences on the *right* of a sequent, much less multisets. After all, doesn't an argument have one conclusion? But the situation is not really any different than having an argument with a set (or a multiset) of premises: we just need to know how to take many conclusions *together*. The standard approach, which we work with here, is this: just as we take a group of premises more-or-less *conjunctively*, so that having A and B as premises is like having "A and B" as a premise, we take a group of conclusions more-or-less *disjunctively*, so that having A and B as conclusions is like having "A or B" as a conclusion. (You may want to practice with this way of thinking by examining the rules we will describe: the rules for $\neg$, and the rule KR, are particularly revealing cases.)

Each piece of vocabulary in the language is subject to two rules: one to say how it is to be used in premises, and one to say how it is

---

[1] A multiset is like a set, except that it pays attention to how many times a formula occurs in it. So while the set $\{A, A, B\}$ is the very same set as $\{A, B\}$, the multiset $[A, A, B]$ is a different multiset from $[A, B]$. Like sets, though, multisets pay no attention to order: the multiset $[A, A, B]$ is the very same multiset as $[A, B, A]$.

[2] We won't discuss nonreflexive substructural approaches to paradox here, but they are certainly possible.

to be used in conclusions. Here, we'll present the rules, and then go on to consider some example derivations. For negation, these are the rules we'll use:

$$\frac{\Gamma : A, \Delta}{\Gamma, \neg A : \Delta} \; \neg L \qquad \frac{\Gamma, A : \Delta}{\Gamma : \neg A, \Delta} \; \neg R$$

To see how to read a rule like this, consider the rule $\neg L$. It tells us that when we have already derived a sequent $\Gamma : A, \Delta$— that is, any sequent that includes at least one occurrence of the formula A among its conclusions—then we may use the rule to derive $\Gamma, \neg A : \Delta$. This sequent differs from the original sequent by including one more occurrence of the formula $\neg A$ among its premises and one less occurrence of A among its conclusions. The other rule, $\neg R$, can be read similarly.

For conjunction, we again have two rules:

$$\frac{\Gamma, A/B : \Delta}{\Gamma, A \wedge B : \Delta} \; \wedge L \qquad \frac{\Gamma : A, \Delta \quad \Gamma : B, \Delta}{\Gamma : A \wedge B, \Delta} \; \wedge R$$

Here, the A/B in the top sequent of $\wedge L$ means that we can apply the rule when either A or B occurs there, replacing one such occurrence with an occurrence of $A \wedge B$. The two sequents on the top of $\wedge R$ means that we must derive sequents of both forms before we can apply the rule. (Note that Γ and Δ in these sequents must match.)

Finally, we need to add rules to cover our (transparent) truth predicate, ensuring that A and $T\langle A \rangle$ are intersubstitutable everywhere. The following pair of rules does the trick:

$$\frac{\Gamma, A : \Delta}{\Gamma, T\langle A \rangle : \Delta} \; TL \qquad \frac{\Gamma : A, \Delta}{\Gamma : T\langle A \rangle, \Delta} \; TR$$

Notice the first of these, though it starts with A and goes to $T\langle A \rangle$, works a lot like release, since it tells you that if you already know how to get somewhere with A as a premise, you can get there with $T\langle A\rangle$ as a premise. The second rule is more like capture, as it tells us that if we can get to A, we can get to $T\langle A\rangle$.

Since the only special vocabulary we're considering is $\neg$, $\wedge$, and T, those are all the vocabulary-specific rules (called *operational rules*) we need. But there are a few more rules we must consider. These rules don't involve any particular vocabulary. Instead, they work on any vocabulary at all. They're called *structural rules*, since they affect the structure of the entire consequence relation, and our substructural approaches will work by fiddling with them.

The first structural rules we consider allow us to add extra premises or conclusions wherever we choose. They are known as *weakening* rules, and usually abbreviated with a K:

$$\frac{\Gamma:\Delta}{\Gamma,A:\Delta}\ KL \qquad \frac{\Gamma:\Delta}{\Gamma:A,\Delta}\ KR$$

The next structural rules allow us to collapse multiple occurrences of the same formula. These are known as *contraction* rules, and abbreviated with a W:

$$\frac{\Gamma,A,A:\Delta}{\Gamma,A:\Delta}\ WL \qquad \frac{\Gamma:A,A,\Delta}{\Gamma:A,\Delta}\ WR$$

The final structural rule we consider allows us to combine two derivations. If we have derived a sequent that includes A as a conclusion and another sequent that includes A as a premise, then we can stick those two sequents together—removing one occurrence of A from each—via this rule, which is known as *cut*:

$$\frac{\Gamma:A,\Delta \quad \Gamma',A:\Delta'}{\Gamma,\Gamma':\Delta,\Delta'}\ Cut$$

Those are all the rules we need to present the approaches we'll consider here. If we take all these rules other than the T rules, we get classical logic.[3] As an example, here is a derivation of *explosion*:

$$
\frac{
  \dfrac{
    \dfrac{
      \dfrac{
        \dfrac{
          \dfrac{A : A}{\neg A, A :}\ \neg L
        }{A \wedge \neg A, A :}\ \wedge L
      }{A \wedge \neg A, A \wedge \neg A :}\ \wedge L
    }{A \wedge \neg A :}\ WL
  }{A \wedge \neg A : B}\ KR
}{}
$$

But unfortunately, we can't add the T rules to all of the others. Together, they would allow us to derive any sequent we like, in the presence of a Liar sentence. Let λ be $\neg T\langle\lambda\rangle$, as usual. Then we have the following derivation of the empty sequent:

$$
\frac{
  \dfrac{
    \dfrac{
      \dfrac{\lambda : \lambda}{T\langle\lambda\rangle : \lambda}\ TL
    }{: \lambda, \neg T\langle\lambda\rangle}\ \neg R
  }{: \lambda}\ WR
  \qquad
  \dfrac{
    \dfrac{
      \dfrac{\lambda : \lambda}{\lambda : T\langle\lambda\rangle}\ TR
    }{\neg T\langle\lambda\rangle, \lambda :}\ \neg L
  }{\lambda :}\ WL
}{:}\ Cut
$$

But any sequent at all can be derived from the empty sequent, by multiple applications of KL and KR. So, if we adopt all of these rules, we must say that every argument whatsoever is valid: a Very Bad result. Just as we saw in Chapter 3, we have to do something to avoid this, lest our worst nightmares, along with our best dreams, follow. (Note that this result depends not at all on the rules for $\wedge$: as you might have expected, conjunction is innocent when it comes to the Liar paradox. The present setting helps reveal this—what our initial derivation in §3.1.3.3 obscured.)

---

[3] This way of presenting a logical system comes from Gentzen (1969). It is useful for many purposes besides those we address here; for example, Gentzen used it to prove the consistency of Peano arithmetic. In addition, there are ways to formulate a sequent system for full classical logic (such as Gentzen's own) so that merely restricting the sequents to those with at most one formula on the right, results in intuitionistic logic.

7.3 Going substructural

The non-classical approaches we have already seen fit into this framework as well. The *paraconsistent* approach rejects the rule ¬L, and the *paracomplete* approach rejects the rule ¬R. These approaches modify the classical theory of negation, and in that way, defuse the Liar paradox. The classical approaches fit in differently, as they reject the rules for T in various ways. (All these approaches do not simply reject these rules; they also add on replacements of various sorts.)

The substructural approaches we'll consider here, though, don't change any of the classical operational rules, or the T rules. Rather, they reject some of the structural rules. The *nontransitive* approach we'll consider instead rejects the rule of cut,[4] and the *noncontractive* approach rejects the rules of contraction. All the other rules we've listed remain in full force on each approach.[5]

Note that this derivation of the empty sequent does not go through in either of these systems; it depends crucially on both contraction and cut. (Although the derivation we've given uses both *WL* and *WR*, in fact either one of these is sufficient to derive the empty sequent, in the presence of cut. Because of this, the noncontractive approach does without both contraction rules.) But it is not only this one derivation. In fact, these substructural

---

[4] Note that cut ensures *transitivity* of consequence; by cutting $B : A$ and $A : C$ together, we can reach $B : C$. Cut is actually stronger than simple transitivity, though. For an approach to paradox that threads the needle, rejecting cut while holding to simple transitivity, see Weir (2005).

[5] You might wonder about rejecting *weakening* instead. If we don't have the K rules, would it really be so bad to derive the empty sequent? But it turns out that an approach like this would still run into trouble when it comes to Curry paradoxes. We won't go into substructural approaches to Curry paradoxes in any detail here; see Restall (1994) for more.

systems turn out to be fully safe; they do not allow for any derivation at all of the empty sequent. Getting rid of one of cut or contraction is enough to guarantee this.

On this kind of nontransitive approach, then, both $\vdash \lambda$ and $\lambda \vdash$ are derivable; the Liar sentence is both a theorem (it follows from anything) and refutable (anything follows from it). But without cut, this fact does not cause the trouble it would usually lead to. On this kind of noncontractive approach, both $\vdash \lambda, \lambda$ and $\lambda, \lambda \vdash$ are derivable: the Liar sentence is not quite a theorem and not quite refutable, but the pair of it with itself follows from anything, and anything follows from the pair of it with itself.[6] If we could contract either of these, then we could get to the empty sequent via cut. But without contraction, we remain safe.

7.4 Advantages

These substructural systems, then, provide a different sort of logical environment in which a transparent truth predicate can happily live. Here, we see just how happy it can be; in the next subsection, we turn to some challenges.

We mentioned previously that, without the truth rules, the system we have presented (that is, including the other operational rules together with the structural rules) determines full classical logic. This allows us to specify a sense in which substructural approaches preserve the classical behavior of the connectives: the operational rules governing $\neg$ and $\wedge$ on these approaches are the very same operational rules that govern these connectives

[6] Although it might sound like it, this final idea is *not* a failure of transitivity: Remember, multiple conclusions are interpreted disjunctively, and multiple premises conjunctively. The pair of λ with itself, then, is not really a single thing at all; the pairing means different things on different sides of the sequent.

classically. (As we mentioned, this is not so for the other non-classical approaches we've considered, which modify the rules for ¬.) Moreover, when the approaches are developed fully, this extends to the other vocabulary as well. So, there is no need, for example, to use a non-classical conditional to deal with Curry paradoxes.

To many people, there seems to be something in common among truth-theoretic paradoxes. Substructural approaches give a theory of just what this is: to the noncontractivist, it's the faulty assumption that contraction always holds; and to the non-transitivist, it's the faulty assumption that cut always holds. By contrast, non-classical theorists seem to need to say that sometimes the trouble is with negation, sometimes it's with the conditional, and sometimes it's something else.[7] There is thus an appealing unity to substructural approaches.

Of course, this appealing unity also holds for the classical approaches we've discussed previously. For these approaches, it is faulty assumptions about truth that are uniformly to blame.[8] But substructural approaches have a different advantage over these classical approaches. Substructural approaches can maintain that truth is fully transparent, come what may, and they can allow for the formation of all kinds of paradoxical sentences. So, the appealing unity exhibited by substructural approaches does not come at the cost of giving up intuitive claims about the truth predicate or self-reference.

---

[7] For a truth-theoretic paradox involving neither negation nor a conditional, see Restall (2013). Related paradoxes arise around the notion of validity, as well, without appeal to negation or a conditional (or a truth predicate!) (e.g., Beall and Murzi, 2013; Shapiro, 2011). Substructural approaches deal with these paradoxes directly, since they too depend on both cut and contraction.

[8] At least if we ignore the validity-theoretic paradoxes mentioned in footnote 7.

Moreover, these substructural approaches, unlike any of the other approaches we've seen, can maintain the appealing claim that valid arguments are truth-preserving, expressed in the object language itself. To present this in detail would require introducing validity predicates and conditionals into the language; rather than do that, we simply refer you to Ripley (2013), where the point is made for a nontransitive approach, and Beall and Murzi (2013), where the point is made for a noncontractive one. Discussion in Shapiro (2013) is also relevant.

Without contraction rules, the consequence relation endorsed by the noncontractivist is not quite classical. For example, there is no derivation anymore of explosion. There is only "almost-explosion": we can derive $A \wedge \neg A, A \wedge \neg A : B$. Similarly, when $\vee$ is added to such an approach, there is no way to derive the law of excluded middle. There is only "almost-excluded middle": $B : A \vee \neg A, A \vee \neg A$. But even the maintaining of almost-explosion and almost-excluded middle leaves us closer to classical consequence than the non-classical approaches considered in Chapter 5, which do not have even this "almost" feature.[9]

Interestingly enough, though, things play differently for the nontransitive approach. Without the truth rules, the very same sequents are derivable whether we include cut as a rule or not.[10] So the system that includes all of our rules other than cut and the truth rules still determines full classical logic. And, of course, adding rules to a system only allows for more things to be derived;

[9] For more precise discussion of some things this 'almost' might amount to, see French and Ripley (2015); Mares and Paoli (2014). There are also other options for conjunction and disjunction in a noncontractive setting. For example, Zardini (2011) prefers a conjunction & that really does give explosion; in Zardini's system, $A \& \neg A \vdash B$. The non-classicality surfaces elsewhere, as $A \nvdash A \& A$ in this system.

[10] Cut still provides useful shortcuts, though: without cut, sometimes the shortest derivation of a sequent is very much longer than it would be with cut (Boolos, 1984).

it never takes anything away. So, the nontransitive system, which includes the truth rules but not the cut rule, allows us to secure the validity of any classically-valid argument. Like its noncontractive relative, it includes a fully transparent truth predicate. This is the sense in which the nontransitive approach combines classical logic with a transparent truth predicate; its consequence relation validates every classically-valid argument, over the full vocabulary (T included).

7.5 Common objections

The most pressing objection faced by substructural approaches, we think, is the following: just what can consequence *be*, such that it does not obey cut or contraction? Although these approaches can derive the object-language claim that valid arguments are truth-preserving, it can be challenging to see how a substructuralist could really understand validity as truth-preservation. The challenge for the nontransitivist is that, at least on the usual way of understanding it, preservation is transitive. The challenge for the noncontractivist is to explain how one occurrence of A can be true without all other occurrences of it being true as well; truth is often thought of as applying to types rather than tokens (or at least to types relative to a context that is supposed to be held fixed).

Here different substructuralists take different tacks. Some, like Ripley (2013); Weir (2005) for a nontransitive approach and Beall

---

Still, there is no difference in which sequents are derivable. Indeed, sequent calculi were developed precisely in order to prove the redundancy of cut, from which a number of interesting and useful properties follow. See again Gentzen (1969) or Negri and von Plato (2001); Troelstra and Schwichtenberg (2000). The basic idea is that as many as possible of the features that make a calculus difficult to work with are distilled into the cut rule. Once we see that cut is redundant, then, we can simply remove it, and avoid these difficulties.

and Murzi (2013); Mares and Paoli (2014) for noncontractive ones, avoid an account of validity as truth-preservation altogether, and give a different kind of theory. Others, like Cobreros *et al.* (2013) for a nontransitive approach and Zardini (2013) for a noncontractive one, consider an account of validity as truth-preservation, but understood in such a way that cut and contraction are not automatically obeyed. We cannot explore these views here, but we record our view that the issue is a pressing one.

Another challenge for substructural views is had in common with the non-classical views of Chapter 5: they seem to deprive us, as reasoners, of at least some of the tools we value. This challenge takes a distinctive form here. We often, it seems, reason in the following way: starting from a bunch of premises, we draw a conclusion. Then, we go on to add that conclusion to our starting premises, forming an expanded base from which to reason. Finally, we go on to draw more conclusions from this newly expanded base. At the end, we count ourselves as having reached our final conclusion from our original premises. Call this *cumulative reasoning*. Of course, we might make a mistake in drawing a conclusion from a certain base of premises, but it might seem that that is the only risk involved in cumulative reasoning: that as long as the conclusions we draw genuinely do follow from our premises, cumulative reasoning itself introduces no further risk. Our eventual conclusion, no matter how many steps it takes to reach it, must follow from our original stock of premises.

Both substructural approaches we've considered here, though, must reject this appearance. Cumulative reasoning, even when its component arguments are valid, introduces the risk of overall invalidity, on both of these approaches. The problem comes in at the step where we add our first conclusion back into our premises to form an expanded bunch of premises.

For the nontransitivist, the problem is that being validly concludable is simply not strong enough to guarantee that a claim can be drawn on as a premise. Transitivity, after all, encodes precisely this assumption; to reject transitivity is to allow that it might fail. For example, in the nontransitive logic we've presented here, λ follows from A, for any A. But B follows from A together with λ, for any B, since anything at all follows from λ. So, if we were to reason cumulatively along this path, we could reach any B from any A.

For the noncontractivist, the problem is slightly different. There is no trouble with taking our first conclusion to be established securely enough to be drawn on as a premise. Instead, the problem is in *keeping* the original premises alive for the second argument. Our first conclusion may have depended on some of the original premises. If we hang on to those premises, and appeal to both them and the first conclusion as well, then we have implicitly appealed to these premises *twice*. But this is just what giving up contraction is supposed to prevent.

The simplest way to see this is to consider a Curry sentence κ that is $T\langle \kappa \rangle \to \bot$, for some robust conditional $\to$. In a noncontractive approach, as you might expect, $\kappa, \kappa \vdash \bot$, but $\kappa \nvdash \bot$. This is crucial for avoiding triviality; if the noncontractivist were to allow $\kappa \vdash \bot$, their theory would turn out to be trivial. So, if we reason from the premise κ alone, we had better not be able to reach $\bot$. Unfortunately, reasoning cumulatively through only noncontractively acceptable arguments, we can. Starting from κ, we can easily reach $T\langle \kappa \rangle \to \bot$; after all, that's just an instance of reflexivity. But if we now add that conclusion back to our initial stock of premises, we have as premises both κ and $T\langle \kappa \rangle \to \bot$; together, by transparency and modus ponens, this is enough to validly conclude $\bot$. So the noncontractivist too must insist that cumulative reasoning can introduce error, even when its component arguments are perfectly valid.

Cumulative reasoning, though, is a very common practice; it would be a shame to have to do without it completely. So substructuralist theories owe us either some replacement, or at the very least some reassurance that we will still be able to reason effectively somehow. Indeed, they can offer such replacements. A nontransitivist should point to the wide range of arguments that can be validated without appeal to transitivity. As we mentioned, this includes *every* classically-valid argument. So, according to the nontransitivist, we can still safely reason cumulatively so long as we stay within this familiar classical range. It is only when we are appealing to the transparency of truth that more care is necessary.

A noncontractivist, on the other hand, should point to something quite like cumulative reasoning: a variant that *throws out* premises once they have been appealed to, but still allows for validly concluded claims to be added to the stock of premises. By removing premises that have been appealed to, and keeping those that have not yet been, the noncontractivist can ensure that there is no risk. This is not full cumulative reasoning, but it is clearly in the ballpark. Whether either or both of these responses are in fact satisfactory is an issue we won't enter into here, except to note that it probably depends on just how much can be recovered through these replacement routes.

As we mentioned in Chapter 5, one way to ask if we have preserved enough of what seems intuitively to be good reasoning is to ask if we can validate the mathematics that goes into our meta-theories, as well as other common mathematical resources. As with the non-classical meta-theories we mentioned in §5.4.1, it is still not entirely clear just how much mathematics can be developed in a contraction-free setting, although see e.g., Petersen (2000); Restall (1994); Weber (2012) for forays.

The situation regarding some nontransitive approaches is clearer, particularly those that validate full classical logic, even in the presence of a truth predicate or paradoxical sentences. Transitive uses of classical logic are not undermined, on these approaches, by the mere appearance of a T in the reasoning (or, for that matter, by the mere appearance of a Liar sentence). It is only if use is actually made of T's transparency (either of the rules TL, TR) that transitivity is put at risk. But no part of classical mathematics has made use of this transparency—so it all carries over into the nontransitive setting as it is.

CHAPTER EIGHT

Other Directions

Revision and Inconsistency

We have now seen some representative samples of approaches to formal theories of truth. In this chapter, we will briefly examine two more approaches that challenge assumptions that are common to all the approaches we have considered so far.

8.1 Inconsistency views

One way to think about the paradoxes, implicit in much of our discussion so far, is this: of course, the languages we speak contain enough self-referential machinery to form paradoxical sentences of all sorts. Nonetheless, all is somehow well: our language manages to be both meaningful and nontrivial, does not force us into falsehoods, etc. In this way of framing the issue, the puzzle is to figure out how this can be so—or, given the wide range of possible ways this could be, some of which we've outlined, to figure out which of those possible ways is actual. How *does* our language manage to avoid disaster, given the existence of paradoxical sentences? Is it not governed by classical logic? Is the intuitive theory of the truth predicate mistaken? How is all well?

So-called *inconsistency* theories reject important aspects of this framing. According to these theories, all is *not* well; the paradoxes *do* in fact cause problems of the sort that is usually assumed off the table. Just which problems they cause is a matter of some controversy among inconsistency theorists. According to Patterson (2007, 2009), for example, there is no true semantic theory describing the meanings of our sentences. According to Azzouni (2007), natural languages are trivial: every sentence in them is true. Other inconsistency theorists are less radical, but still claim that something is amiss: according to Eklund (2002), competence with "true" requires us to be disposed to accept every instance of the T-schema, even though (infinitely) many of those instances are false. According to Scharp (2013), *true* is an inconsistent concept, like the prerelativistic concept *mass*, and so unsuitable for careful theorizing. According to Armour-Garb and Woodbridge (2015) and (perhaps) Burgess and Burgess (2011),[1] nothing at all is *really* true, although we might want to pretend that some things are. According to Badici and Ludwig (2007), "true" does not have a meaning. And so on.[2]

We won't sort through the debates among these views here, but we do want to call attention to the wide variety of claims captured under the single heading "inconsistency views". There is probably no single statement of inconsistency views that would be acceptable to all parties. Despite this variety, there is something of a family resemblance among these views; all try to take seriously the possibility that the paradoxical derivations really do go through

[1] Burgess and Burgess discuss the view but fall short of endorsing it. One of the Burgesses discusses this further in Burgess (2017).
[2] Inconsistency theories of truth go back at least to Tarski (though interpretation of Tarski remains contentious). Chihara (1979); Mates (1981) are also often cited as early statements. In the current century, though, they have received more sustained exploration than before.

in the language we speak, that our language as it is is in some way disordered as a result of the paradoxes.

Such views thus have a ready answer to an important kind of question that naturally arises around paradoxes of all sorts: why did we fall for the paradox in the first place? (In an influential discussion of vagueness, Fara (2000) calls the analogue of this the "psychological question.") Any theorist who claims that the paradoxical derivations fail, for whatever reason, is making a quite counterintuitive claim. After all, every step in the paradoxical derivations looks good, and they seem to be put together in the right sort of ways. (That's why there's a problem in the first place!) The intuition the claim goes against is itself part of what's to be explained. Someone who thinks that explosion doesn't really preserve truth, or that truth doesn't really obey capture and release, or that cut doesn't really preserve validity, or whatever, owes some explanation as to why we initially thought it did.

Inconsistency theorists, though, build their theory in the first place around some sense in which the paradoxical derivations *succeed*. Just what any particular inconsistency theorist will say depends on the particular sense in which that theorist takes the derivations to succeed, but in general the sense will provide an answer to the psychological question. Indeed, the literature on inconsistency views contains rich sustained discussion of the psychological question with respect to the Liar paradox (e.g., Eklund, 2002; Patterson, 2007, 2009; Scharp, 2013).

8.1.1 Now what?

Inconsistency views are sometimes presented, even by their proponents, as a form of defeatism (e.g., Burgess and Burgess, 2011).

The idea is presumably that they have given up on the idea that all is well as it is. But there is no need to cast them in such a sour-faced mould. There is a natural place in inconsistency views for optimism of a certain sort: not optimism about how things *are*, but instead optimism about *potential reform*.[3] Although inconsistency views might say that something is rotten in the state of Danish (and other natural languages), they are not obliged to conclude that this is unavoidable. This provides another dimension of variation among inconsistency views. Given that we find ourselves speaking an inconsistent language (in whatever sense), what are we to do about it?

One possibility is: nothing. This kind of view would have it that there is simply no trouble at all in using an inconsistent language. Perhaps we ought to change our beliefs *about* the language we speak (at least if we don't already recognize it as inconsistent), but there is no need for change in the language itself. Views like this seem to be defended by Eklund (2002); Patterson (2007, 2009).

Another possibility is: throw out the inconsistent language and find a consistent one. This kind of view would have it that there is something misguided about using an inconsistent language. This could perhaps be underwritten by claims about the goals that language use serves, together with some argument that an inconsistent language cannot serve those goals. But, at least if combined with the view that natural languages are in fact inconsistent, it would seem to lack a certain sort of philosophical modesty currently in vogue. As far as we know, no inconsistency theorist has recommended such a view.

[3] This division tracks Scharp's (2013) division between the "descriptive" and "normative" parts of an inconsistency theory.

The majority of inconsistency theorists aim between these two extremes, recommending that we change our linguistic practices *for some purposes*, or *in some contexts*, without calling for total revision. Exactly which purposes are thought to call for revision vary from theorist to theorist. Views like this seem to be defended by Azzouni (2007); Badici and Ludwig (2007); Burgess and Burgess (2011); Scharp (2013).

8.1.2 *Relations to other views*

On any view that recommend revision of existing practice, whether total or partial, there is an obvious further question: *how* should existing practice be revised? Here, too, inconsistency theorists differ from each other. We want to call attention to an easy-to-overlook point: inconsistency theorists facing this question can and should help themselves to work that's already been done for them by other theorists.

To be sure, we are not the first to make something like this point. For example, Badici and Ludwig say:

> [V]arious proposals which have been made about the actual semantics of the truth predicate which are designed to show that the semantic principles attaching to it are sophisticated enough to avoid any difficulties are better thought of as instructions for how to revise the language self-consciously so as to avoid the difficulties into which we have fallen   (Badici and Ludwig, 2007, p. 631).

In fact, though, inconsistency theorists tend to offer recommended revisions of a very particular sort: revisions that hold to strongly classical logic but do not hold to both capture and release. (You can see a sign of this in the previous quote, where Badici and Ludwig only consider proposals about the "semantics of the truth predicate.") But this seems arbitrary: they are as free to recommend revision in the principles they take to govern negation, for example, as they are to recommend revision in the principles they take to govern "true."

Moreover, the reasons that might be offered for revising "true" rather than "not," or for revising "not" rather than "true," would seem not to be far off from the reasons that have in fact been offered by consistency theorists for thinking that our language in fact does not contain a naive truth predicate, or does not contain a classical negation. These reasons are quite often about our goals in language use, and how they would be best served: reasons that carry over nicely into discussion of potential revisions.

8.1.3 Objections

The most obvious objection to inconsistency theories in general is perhaps best stated in Wittgenstein (1967, Paragraph 98): ". . . it is clear that every sentence in our language 'is in order as it is.' " It is just *obvious*, for example, that our language is not meaningless, or that not every sentence in our language is true. But this impression of obviousness can fade when we look to less radical inconsistency theories; is it really *obvious* that our competence with the word "true" commits us to nothing false?

Arguments in favor of inconsistency views tend to center around derivations like the one of §3.1.3.3. So any way of undermining such a derivation—and we have seen plenty in this book—can serve as a way of undermining the main support for inconsistency views. This is no objection to such views themselves, but makes it clear just how difficult it is to convincingly support an inconsistency view in this way. One would have to reject all the other views we have surveyed to think that this derivation actually succeeds.

8.2 The revision theory of truth

According to the *revision theory*, developed by Gupta (1982); Gupta and Belnap (1993); Herzberger (1982), and a number of others, the right approach to truth is to see it as a *circular concept*: one with a circular definition. Although traditional theories of definition ban circular definitions, revision theories go some way to rehabilitating them, showing how rich they can be if taken seriously. The revision theory's approach to circular concepts is to see them not as determining an extension, but rather as providing a rule for how to modify, or revise, extensions.[4] A circular concept might seem to give inconsistent verdicts on what falls under it. For example, if truth is defined via the T-schema, the Liar comes out true, and so untrue, and so true, and so untrue.... Revision theory, however, sees it as giving one verdict *at a time*; truth and untruth here do not clash because they are never *simultaneously* present; they rather endlessly supplant each other.[5] In some cases, like the case of truth, we wind up making such changes in a never-ending sequence. It is these sequences, known as revision sequences, that the revision theory studies.

8.2.1 FORMAL PICTURE

We will illustrate this with a basic application of the revision theory to truth predicates. Start, as we have before, with a classical language $\mathcal{L}^+$ with a truth predicate T. Unlike other classical

---

[4] The connection between the revision theory and circular concepts is highlighted in Gupta and Belnap (1993). For a discussion of the foundations of the revision theory, and its relations to contextualism and inconsistency theories, see Shapiro (2006); Yablo (1993a). Some of the many developments in the revision theory are reported in Chapuis and Gupta (2000).

[5] For similar reflections on instability in a different logical setting, see Zardini (2011).

frameworks, we will make use of unrestricted capture and release. However, we will not make use of these by assuming that they hold; rather, we will use them to guide our revisions. We pick a set H to be the extension of T, and form a model of $\mathcal{L}^+$ by adding H to a model of $\mathcal{L}$. H is a *hypothesis* about what the extension of T might be. H may be $\emptyset$, it may be the entire domain D, or it may be anything else. It need not be a particularly good approximation of the semantic properties of T.

Although the T-schema cannot hold in $\langle \mathfrak{M}, H \rangle$, the model still gives us an interpretation of $\mathcal{L}^+$. Thus, we can ask which sentences of $\mathcal{L}^+$ are true in this model. Let $\tau(H) = \{\langle A \rangle : \langle \mathfrak{M}, H \rangle \models A\}$. Revision theorists claim that $\tau(H)$ is often a "better" hypothesis about the extension of T than H was. We can then form the model $\langle \mathfrak{M}, \tau(H) \rangle$ for $\mathcal{L}^+$. This is something like "applying the T-schema to $\mathcal{L}^+$," relative to the hypothesis H about the interpretation of T.[6]

When it comes to sentences like λ, the "improvement" in our hypothesis is unstable. Each iteration of τ will lead to a change in the status of λ. As a starting hypothesis, let us consider $H = \emptyset$. Consider what happens to the truth of λ as we apply τ:

n	truth value of λ in $\langle \mathcal{M}_0, \tau^n(\emptyset) \rangle$
0	true
1	false
2	true
3	false
4	true
$\vdots$	$\vdots$

[6] Of course, the T-schema itself isn't really the kind of thing that can be applied—but this is one intuitive way to see what's going on here. One way to cash out this idea is explored in Standefer and Gupta (2017).

The Liar sentence never stabilizes under this process. We reach an alternation of truth values which will go on for ever.

In the terminology of the revision theory, τ is a *revision rule*. It takes us from one hypothesis about the interpretation of T to another. Sequences of values generated by such revision rules, starting with a given initial hypothesis, are called *revision sequences*.

The characteristic property of paradoxical sentences like the Liar sentence is that they are unstable in revision sequences: there is no point in the sequence at which they reach a stable truth value. This classifies sentences as stably true, stably false, and unstable. It is possible to develop notions of consequence based on these, and related, notions.[7]

8.2.2 COMMON OBJECTIONS

The revision theory offers us a formal tool for exploring circular concepts. But in doing so, it does something very different from the other approaches we have considered. All the other approaches we have discussed do something we could call giving a "theory" of truth. Some do give axiomatic theories; others give interpreted languages; yet others give hierarchies of such. But each does offer a specific proposal for how truth is to be understood. The revision theory does this only by offering a way to approach revision sequences. It offers no extension for T, nor an axiomatic theory beyond the inconsistent combination of the T-schema and classical logic. Proponents of the revision theory argue that this is the correct way to approach concepts like truth, but others object that it fails to provide what we were seeking in studying truth.

In response, the revision theory does offer some theories of revision sequences. One feature of these theories is that even by

---

[7] See Gupta and Belnap (1993) for more discussion of these issues.

lights of the complex theories we have been considering, these are very complex. In some cases, accurate mathematical measures of their complexity are difficult. This is not an objection per se, but it does illustrate why the revision theory can be somewhat difficult to work with.[8]

Difficult or not, the revision theory has proved a useful tool for more traditional approaches to truth, over and above its use by its proponents. For instance, Field (2008) deploys revision-theoretic techniques to build models for the conditional that is distinctive of the (non-revision-theoretic) approach defended there.

[8] In addition to Gupta and Belnap (1993), see for instance Welch (2001), among others.

CHAPTER NINE

Closing Remarks

You've read this far, and we hope that you enjoyed the ride. Now we must repeat: we have only scratched the surface—if even that— of any of the formal theories of truth we have discussed. Still, we are optimistic that you now have some sense of the wide range of options and approaches for exploring truth and its paradoxes. Some approaches have been more closely linked to natural language, others to mathematics, and others seem to stand more on their own. But all the theories we have considered have this much in common: they use the tools of formal logic to state and explore precise theories about the inferential behavior and semantics of truth, negation, conditionals, and the other vocabulary tangled up in paradox.

The study of truth takes many directions. Some explore the metaphysics of truth, its applications to epistemology, its role in science and mathematics, or other issues. We believe that understanding the basic formal properties of truth, and the issues in logic that go with them, is a good starting place for those many areas of exploration. It is, of course, a good starting place for the rich complexity and variety of formal theories of truth. With the basics we have provided here, you should be ready to swim out to the deep end of the pool.

BIBLIOGRAPHY

Anderson, Alan Ross (1970). St. Paul's epistle to Titus. In *The Paradox of the Liar* (ed. R. L. Martin), pp. 1–11. Ridgeview, Atascadero.

Anderson, Alan Ross and Nuel D. Belnap (1975). *Entailment: The Logic of Relevance and Necessity*, Volume 1. Princeton University Press, Princeton, New Jersey.

Armour-Garb, Bradley and Jc Beall (2001). Can deflationists be dialetheists? *Journal of Philosophical Logic*, 30(6), 593–608.

Armour-Garb, Bradley and Jc Beall (2003). Should deflationists be dialetheists? *Noûs*, 37(2), 303–24.

Armour-Garb, Bradley and James Woodbridge (2015). Truth, pretense and the Liar paradox. In *Unifying the Philosophy of Truth* (ed. T. Achourioti, H. Galinon, J. Martínez Fernández, and K. Fujimoto), pp. 339–454. Springer, Dordrecht.

Asenjo, F. G. (1966). A calculus of antinomies. *Notre Dame Journal of Formal Logic*, 16, 103–5.

Asenjo, F. G. and J. Tamburino (1975). Logic of antinomies. *Notre Dame Journal of Formal Logic*, 16(1), 17–44.

Azzouni, Jody (2007). The inconsistency of natural languages: How we live with it. *Inquiry*, 50(6), 590–605.

Badici, Emil and Kirk Ludwig (2007). The concept of truth and the semantics of the truth predicate. *Inquiry*, 50(6), 622–38.

Barrio, Eduardo A. (2006). Theories of truth without standard models and Yabol's sequences. *Studia Logica*, 82, 1–17.

Barrio, Eduardo A. (2012). The Yablo paradox and circularity. *Análisis Filosófico*, 32(1), 7–20.

Barwise, Jon and John Etchemendy (1987). *The Liar: an Essay on Truth and Circularity*. Oxford University Press, Oxford.

Beall, Jc (2001). Is Yablo's paradox non-circular? *Analysis*, 61, 176–87.

Beall, Jc (2005). Transparent disquotationalism. In *Deflationism and Paradox* (ed. J. Beall and B. Armour-Garb), pp. 7–22. Oxford University Press, Oxford.

Beall, Jc (2008a). Curry's paradox. In *Stanford Encyclopedia of Philosophy* (ed. E. N. Zalta).

Beall, Jc (2008b). Prolegomenon to future revenge. In *Revenge of the Liar* (ed. J. Beall), pp. 1–30. Oxford University Press, Oxford.

Beall, Jc (2009). *Spandrels of Truth*. Oxford University Press, Oxford.

Beall, Jc (2010). *Logic: The Basics*. Routledge, Oxford.

Beall, Jc (2013a). LP^+, $K3^+$, FDE^+ and their classical collapse. *Review of Symbolic Logic*, 6, 742–54.

Beall, Jc (2013b). Shrieking against gluts: the solution to the 'just true' problem. *Analysis*, 73, 438–45.

Beall, Jc (2013c). A simple approach towards recapturing consistent theories in paraconsistent settings. *Review of Symbolic Logic*, 6, 755–64.

Beall, Jc (2015). Free of detachment: logic, rationality, and gluts. *Noûs*, 49, 410–23.

Beall, Jc and Michael Glanzberg (2008). Where the paths meet: Remarks on truth and paradox. In *Midwest Studies in Philosophy Volume XXXII: Truth and its Deformities* (ed. P. A. French and H. K. Wettstein). Wiley-Blackwell, Boston.

Beall, Jc, Michael Hughes and Ross Vandegrift (2014). Glutty theories and the logic of antinomies. In *The Metaphysics of Logic* (ed. P. Rush), pp. 224–32. Cambridge University Press, Cambridge. Also available at Cambridge Books Online via url = dx.doi.org/10.1017/CBO9781139626279.017.

Beall, Jc and Julien Murzi (2013). Two flavors of Curry's paradox. *Journal of Philosophy*, 110(3), 143–65.

Beall, Jc and Greg Restall (2006). *Logical Pluralism*. Oxford University Press, Oxford.

Beall, Jc and David Ripley (2004). Analetheism and dialetheism. *Analysis*, 64(1), 30–5.

Beall, Jc and Bas C. van Fraassen (2003). *Possibilities and Paradox: An Introduction to Modal and Many-valued Logic*. Oxford University Press, Oxford.

Boolos, George S. (1984). Don't eliminate cut. *Journal of Philosophical Logic*, 13(4), 373–8.

Boolos, George S. (1995). *The Logic of Provability*. Cambridge University Press, Cambridge.

Boolos, George S., John P. Burgess and Richard C. Jeffrey (2007). *Computability and Logic* (fifth edn). Cambridge University Press, Cambridge.

Brady, Ross T. (1971). The consistency of the axioms of abstraction and extensionality in a three-valued logic. *Notre Dame Journal of Formal Logic*, 12(4), 447–53.

Brady, Ross T. (1989a). The non-triviality of dialectical set theory. In *Paraconsistent Logic: Essays on the Inconsistent* (ed. G. Priest, R. Routley, and J. Norman), pp. 437–70. Philosophia Verlag, Munich.

Brady, Ross T. (1989b). The non-triviality of dialectical set theory. In *Paraconsistent Logic: Essays on the Inconsistent* (ed. G. Priest, R. Routley, and J. Norman), pp. 437–71. Philosophia Verlag, München.

Brady, Ross T. (2006). *Universal Logic*. CSLI Publications, Stanford, California.

Brady, Ross T. (2011). Metavaluations, naive set theory, and inconsistency. In *Logic Without Frontiers: Festschrift for Walter Alexandre Carnielli on the Occasion of his 60th Birthday* (ed. J.-Y. Beziau and M. E. Coniglio), pp. 339–60. College Publications, London.

Brady, Ross T. (2014). The simple consistency of naive set theory using metavaluations. *Journal of Philosophical Logic*, 43(2–3), 261–81.

Brandom, Robert (1994). *Making It Explicit*. Harvard University Press, Cambridge, Massachusetts.

Burge, Tyler (1979). Semantical paradox. *Journal of Philosophy*, 76, 169–98. Reprinted in Martin (1984).

Burgess, Alexis (2017). Truth in fictionalism. In *Oxford Handbook of Truth* (ed. M. Glanzberg). Oxford University Press, Oxford. Forthcoming.

Burgess, Alexis G. and John P. Burgess (2011). *Truth*. Princeton University Press, Princeton, NJ.

Chapuis, Andre and Gupta, Anil (ed.) (2000). *Circularity, Definition and Truth*. Indian Council of Philosophical Research, New Delhi.

Chihara, Charles (1979). The semantic paradoxes: A diagnostic investigation. *Philosophical Review*, 88, 590–618.

Cobreros, Pablo, Paul Égré, David Ripley, and Robert van Rooij (2013). Reaching transparent truth. *Mind*, 122(488), 841–66.

Cook, Roy T. (2006). There are non-circular paradoxes (but Yablo's isn't one of them). *The Monist*, 89, 118–49.

Cook, Roy T. (2013). *Paradoxes*. Polity, Oxford.

Cook, Roy T. (2014). *The Yablo Paradox: An Essay on Circularity*. Oxford University Press, Oxford.

Dunn, J. Michael (1969). Natural language versus formal language. Unpublished paper presented at the joint APA–ASL symposium, New York, December 27, 1969.

Dunn, J. Michael and Gary M. Hardegree (2001). *Algebraic Methods in Philosophical Logic*. Oxford University Press, Oxford.

Eklund, Matti (2002). Inconsistent languages. *Philosophy and Phenomenological Research*, 64, 251–75.

Fara, Delia Graff (2000). Shifting sands: An interest-relative theory of vagueness. *Philosophical Topics*, 28(1), 45–81. (Originally published under the name "Delia Graff").

Feferman, Solomon (1984). Toward useful type-free theories I. *Journal of Symbolic Logic*, 49(1), 75–111.

Feferman, Solomon (1991). Reflecting on incompleteness. *Journal of Symbolic Logic*, 56, 1–49.

Feferman, Solomon (2008). *Saving Truth from Paradox*. Oxford University Press, Oxford.

Field, Hartry (1994). Deflationist views of meaning and content. *Mind*, 103, 249–85.

Fine, Kit (1974). Models of entailment. *Journal of Philosophical Logic*, 3, 347–72.

French, Rohan and David Ripley (2015). Contractions of noncontractive consequence relations. *Review of Symbolic Logic*, 8, 506–28.

Friedman, Harvey and Michael Sheard (1987). An axiomatic approach to self-referential truth. *Annals of Pure and Applied Logic*, 33, 1–21.

Fujimoto, Kentaro (2011). Autonomous progressions and transfinite iteration of self-applicable truth. *Journal of Symbolic Logic*, 76, 914–45.

Gaifman, Haim (1988). Operational pointer semantics: Solution to self-referential puzzles I. In *Proceedings of the Second Conference on Theoretical Aspects of Reasoning about Knowledge* (ed. M. Y. Vardi), pp. 43–59. Morgan Kaufmann, Los Altos.

Gaifman, Haim (1992). Pointers to truth. *Journal of Philosophy*, 89, 223–261.

Gaifman, Haim (2000). Pointers to propositions. In *Circularity, Definition and Truth* (ed. A. Chapuis and A. Gupta), pp. 79–121. Indian Council of Philosophical Research, New Delhi.

Gauker, Christopher (2006). Against stepping back: A critique of contextualist approaches to the semantic paradoxes. *Journal of Philosophical Logic*, 35, 393–422.

Gentzen, Gerhard (1969). Investigations into logical deduction. In *The Collected Papers of Gerhard Gentzen* (ed. M. E. Szabo), pp. 68–131. North-Holland Publishing Company, Amsterdam.

Glanzberg, Michael (2001). The Liar in context. *Philosophical Studies*, 103, 217–51.

Glanzberg, Michael (2004a). A contextual-hierarchical approach to truth and the Liar paradox. *Journal of Philosophical Logic*, 33, 27–88.

Glanzberg, Michael (2004b). Quantification and realism. *Philosophy and Phenomenological Research*, 69, 541–72.

Glanzberg, Michael (2004c). Truth, reflection, and hierarchies. *Synthese*, 142, 289–315.

Glanzberg, Michael (2006). Context and unrestricted quantification. In *Absolute Generality* (ed. A. Rayo and G. Uzquiano), pp. 45–74. Oxford University Press, Oxford.

Glanzberg, Michael (2015). Complexity and hierarchy in truth predicates. In *Unifying the Philosophy of Truth* (ed. T. Achourioti, H. Galinon, J. Martínez Fernández, and K. Fujimoto), pp. 211–43. Springer, Dordrecht.

Glanzberg, Michael (ed.) (2018). *Oxford Handbook of Truth*. Oxford University Press, Oxford.

Groeneveld, Willem (1994). Dynamic semantics and circular propositions. *Journal of Philosophical Logic*, 23, 267–306.

Gupta, Anil (1982). Truth and paradox. *Journal of Philosophical Logic*, 11, 1–60. Reprinted in Martin (1984).

Gupta, Anil and Nuel Belnap (1993). *The Revision Theory of Truth.* MIT Press, Cambridge, Massachusetts.

Halbach, Volker (1994). A system of complete and consistent truth. *Notre Dame Journal of Formal Logic,* 35, 311–27.

Halbach, Volker (1997). Tarskian and Kripean truth. *Journal of Philosophical Logic,* 26, 69–80.

Halbach, Volker (2011). *Axiomatic Theories of Truth.* Cambridge University Press, Cambridge.

Halbach, Volker and Leon Horsten (2006). Axiomatizing Kripke's theory of truth. *Journal of Symbolic Logic,* 71(2), 677–712.

Heck, Jr., Richard G. (2007). Self-reference and the languages of arithmetic. *Philosophia Mathematica,* 15(1), 1–29.

Herzberger, Hans G. (1970). Paradoxes of grounding in semantics. *Journal of Philosophy,* 67, 146–67.

Herzberger, Hans G. (1982). Notes on naive semantics. *Journal of Philosophical Logic,* 11, 61–102. Reprinted in Martin (1984).

Horsten, Leon (2011). *The Tarskian Turn: Deflationism and Axiomatic Truth.* MIT Press, Cambridge, Massachusetts.

Humberstone, Lloyd (2012). *The Connectives.* MIT Press, Cambridge, Massachusetts.

Hyde, Dominic (1997). From heaps and gaps to heaps of gluts. *Mind,* 106, 641–60.

Jager, Gerhard, Reinhard Kahle, Anton Setzer, and Thomas Strahm (1999). The proof-theoretic analysis of transfinitely iterated fixed point theories. *Journal of Symbolic Logic,* 64, 53–67.

Juhl, Cory F. (1997). A context-sensitive Liar. *Analysis,* 57, 202–4.

Keefe, Rosanna (2000). *Theories of Vagueness.* Cambridge University Press, Cambridge.

Kleene, S. C. (1952). *Introduction to Metamathematics.* North-Holland Publishing Company, Amsterdam.

Koons, Robert C. (1992). *Paradoxes of Belief and Strategic Rationality.* Cambridge University Press, Cambridge.

Kratzer, Angelika (1979). Conditional necessity and possibility. In *Semantics from different points of view* (ed. R. Bäuerle, U. Egli, and A. von Stechow), pp. 117–47. Springer, Heidelberg.

Kremer, Michael (1988). Kripke and the logic of truth. *Journal of Philosophical Logic*, **17**(3), 225–78.

Kripke, Saul (1975). Outline of a theory of truth. *Journal of Philosophy*, **72**(19), 690–716.

Leitgeb, Hannes (2007). What theories of truth should be like (but cannot be). *Philosophy Compass*, **2**, 276–90.

Lewis, Clarence Irving and Cooper H. Langford (1959). *Symbolic Logic*. Dover, Mineola, New York.

McGee, Vann (1991). *Truth, Vagueness, and Paradox*. Hackett, Indianapolis.

Mares, Edwin and Francesco Paoli (2014). Logical consequence and the paradoxes. *Journal of Philosophical Logic*, **43**(2–3), 439–69.

Martin, Robert L. (ed.) (1984). *Recent Essays on Truth and the Liar Paradox*. Oxford University Press, Oxford.

Mates, Benson (1981). *Skeptical Essays*. University of Chicago Press, Chicago.

Maudlin, Tim (2004). *Truth and Paradox*. Oxford University Press, Oxford.

Meadows, Toby (2014). Fixed points for consequence relations. *Logique et Analyse*, **57**, 333–57.

Meyer, Robert K. and Richard Routley (1973). Classical relevant logics I. *Studia Logica*, **32**, 51–68.

Meyer, Robert K. and Richard Routley (1974). Classical relevant logics II. *Studia Logica*, **33**(2), 183–194.

Mortensen, Chris (1995). *Inconsistent Mathematics*. Kluwer Academic Publishers, Dordrecht.

Negri, Sara and Jan von Plato (2001). *Structural Proof Theory*. Cambridge University Press, Cambridge.

Parsons, Charles (1974). The Liar paradox. *Journal of Philosophical Logic*, **3**, 381–412. Reprinted in Parsons (1983).

Parsons, Charles (1983). *Mathematics in Philosophy*. Cornell University Press, Ithaca, New York.

Parsons, Terence (1984). Assertion, denial, and the Liar paradox. *Journal of Philosophical Logic*, **13**, 137–52.

Patterson, Douglas (2007). Understanding the Liar. In *The Revenge of the Liar* (ed. J. Beall), pp. 197–224. Oxford University Press, Oxford.

Patterson, Douglas (2009). Inconsistency theories of semantic paradox. *Philosophy and Phenomenological Research*, 79, 387–422.

Petersen, Uwe (2000). Logic without contraction as based on inclusion and unrestricted abstraction. *Studia Logica*, 64(3), 365–403.

Priest, Graham (1979). Logic of paradox. *Journal of Philosophical Logic*, 8, 219–41.

Priest, Graham (1997). Yablo's paradox. *Analysis*, 57, 236–42.

Priest, Graham (2003). Inconsistent arithmetic: Issues technical and philosophical. In *Trends in Logic: 50 Years of* Studia Logica (ed. V. F. Hendricks and J. Malinowski), pp. 273–99. Kluwer, Dordrecht.

Priest, Graham (2006a). *Doubt Truth to be a Liar*. Oxford University Press, Oxford.

Priest, Graham (2006b). *In Contradiction* (Second edn). Oxford University Press, Oxford. First printed by Martinus Nijhoff in 1987.

Priest, Graham (2008). *An Introduction to Non-Classical Logic: From If to Is* (second edn). Cambridge University Press, Cambridge.

Priest, Graham (2010). Hopes fade for saving truth. *Philosophy*, 85(1), 109–40.

Priest, Graham and Richard Routley (1989). First historical introduction: A preliminary history of paraconsistent and dialetheic approaches. In *Paraconsistent Logic: Essays on the Inconsistent* (ed. G. Priest, R. Routley, and J. Norman), pp. 3–75. Philosophia Verlag, Munich.

Rabern, Landon, Brian Rabern, and Matthew Macauley (2013). Dangerous reference graphs and semantic paradoxes. *Journal of Philosophical Logic*, 42(5), 727–65.

Rahman, Shahid, Tero Tulenheimo, and Emmanuel Genot (ed.) (2008). *Unity, Truth and the Liar: The Modern Relevance of Medieval Solutions to the Liar Paradox*. Springer Verlag, Berlin.

Rayo, Agustín and Gabriel Uzquiano (ed.) (2006). *Absolute Generality*. Oxford University Press, Oxford.

Read, Stephen (2002). The Liar paradox from John Buridan back to Thomas Bradwardine. *Vivarium*, 40, 189–218.

Read, Stephen (2006). Symmetry and paradox. *History and Philosophy of Logic*, 27, 307–18.

Reinhardt, William N. (1986). Some remarks on extending and interpreting theories with a partial predicate for truth. *Journal of Philosophical Logic*, 15, 219–51.

Restall, Greg (1994). *On Logics Without Contraction*. Ph.D. thesis, The University of Queensland.

Restall, Greg (2008). Modal models for Bradwardine's theory of truth. *Review of Symbolic Logic*, 1, 225–40.

Restall, Greg (2013). Assertion, denial, and non-classical theories. In *Paraconsistency: Logic and Applications* (ed. K. Tanaka, F. Berto, E. Mares, and F. Paoli), pp. 81–100. Springer, Dordrecht.

Ripley, David (2012). Conservatively extending classical logic with transparent truth. *Review of Symbolic Logic*, 5(2), 354–78.

Ripley, David (2013). Paradoxes and failures of cut. *Australasian Journal of Philosophy*, 91(1), 139–64.

Ripley, David (2015). Embedding denial. In *Foundations of Logical Consequence* (ed. C. R. Caret and O. T. Hjortland), pp. 289–309. Oxford University Press, Oxford.

Routley, Richard (1979). Dialectical logic, semantics and metamathematics. *Erkenntnis*, 14, 301–31.

Routley, Richard, Robert K. Meyer, Val Plumwood, and Ross T. Brady (1982). *Relevant Logics and their Rivals 1*. Ridgeview, Atascadero, California.

Sainsbury, R.M. (2009). *Paradoxes* (Third edn). Cambridge University Press, Cambridge.

Scharp, Kevin (2013). *Replacing Truth*. Oxford University Press, Oxford.

Shapiro, Lionel (2006). The rationale behind the revision theory. *Philosophical Studies*, 129, 477–515.

Shapiro, Lionel (2011). Deflating logical consequence. *Philosophical Quarterly*, 61(243), 320–42.

Shapiro, Lionel (2013). Validity Curry strengthened. *Thought*, 2(2), 100–7.

Shapiro, Stewart (2004). Simple truth, contradiction, and consistency. In *The Law of Non-Contradiction* (ed. G. Priest, J. Beall, and B. Armour-Garb), pp. 336–54. Oxford University Press, Oxford.

Simmons, Keith (1993). *Universality and the Liar*. Cambridge University Press, Cambridge.

Simmons, Keith (2018). Contextual theories of truth. In *Oxford Handbook of Truth* (ed. M. Glanzberg). Oxford University Press, Oxford. Forthcoming.

Smith, Peter (2007). *An Introduction to Gödel's Theorems*. Cambridge University Press, Cambridge.

Soames, Scott (1999). *Understanding Truth*. Oxford University Press, Oxford.

Sorensen, Roy (1998). Yablo's paradox and kindred infinite Liars. *Mind*, **107**, 137–55.

Sorensen, Roy (2003). *A Brief History of Paradox*. Oxford University Press, Oxford.

Standefer, Shawn and Anil Gupta (2017). Conditionals in theories of truth. Journal of Philosophical Logic, **46**, 27–63.

Tarski, Alfred (1935). Der Wahrheitsbegriff in den formalizierten Sprachen. *Studia Philosophica*, **1**, 261–405. References are to the translation by J. H. Woodger as "The concept of truth in formalized languages" in Tarski (1983).

Tarski, Alfred (1944). The semantic conception of truth. *Philosophy and Phenomenological Research*, **4**, 341–76.

Tarski, Alfred (1983). *Logic, Semantics, Metamathematics* (Second edn). Hackett, Indianapolis. Edited by J. Corcoran with translations by J. H. Woodger.

Troelstra, Anne Sjerp and Helmut Schwichtenberg (2000). *Basic Proof Theory* (Second edn). Cambridge University Press, Cambridge.

van Fraassen, Bas C. (1966). Singular terms, truth-value gaps and free logic. *Journal of Philosophy*, **63**, 481–95.

van Fraassen, Bas C. (1968). Presupposition, implication, and self-reference. *Journal of Philosophy*, **65**, 136–52.

Visser, Albert (1984). Four valued semantics and the Liar. *Journal of Philosophical Logic*, **13**, 181–212.

Weber, Zach (2012). Transfinite cardinals in paraconsistent set theory. *Review of Symbolic Logic*, **5**(2), 269–93.

Weir, Alan (2005). Naïve truth and sophisticated logic. In *Deflationism and Paradox* (ed. J. Beall and B. Armour-Garb), pp. 218–49. Oxford University Press, Oxford.

Welch, Philip D. (2001). On Gupta–Belnap revision theories of truth, Kripkean fixed points, and the next stable set. *Bulletin of Symbolic Logic*, 7, 345–60.

Welch, Philip D. (2008). Ultimate truth *vis-à-vis* stable truth. *Review of Symbolic Logic*, 1(1), 126–42.

Williamson, Timothy (1994). *Vagueness*. Routledge, London.

Wittgenstein, Ludwig (1967). *Philosophical Investigations*. Blackwell. Translated by G. E. M. Anscombe.

Woodruff, Peter W. (1984). Paradox, truth, and logic part 1: Paradox and truth. *Journal of Philosophical Logic*, 13, 213–32.

Yablo, Stephen (1993a). Hop, skip, and jump: The agonistic conception of truth. *Philosophical Perspectives*, 7, 371–96.

Yablo, Stephen (1993b). Paradox without self-reference. *Analysis*, 53, 251–2.

Zardini, Elia (2011). Truth without contra(di)ction. *Review of Symbolic Logic*, 4(4), 498–535.

Zardini, Elia (2013). Naive modus ponens. *Journal of Philosophical Logic*, 42(4), 575–93.

NAME INDEX

GENERAL INDEX